HOW TO STOP **OVERTHINKING**

11 Biblical Secrets to Letting Go of Negative Thinking, Anxiety, and Stress

MIKE VESTIL

Published by MONTMADA LLC

This book is a work of nonfiction. While it draws from historical, cultural, philosophical, and spiritual frameworks, it is intended solely for educational and inspirational purposes. The insights, reflections, and suggestions herein are based on the author's personal experiences, research, and interpretations.

The author is not a licensed therapist, counselor, psychologist, psychiatrist, medical doctor, or legal professional. Nothing in this book should be considered or used as a substitute for medical, psychological, psychiatric, therapeutic, financial, or legal advice. Always seek the advice of a qualified healthcare provider, licensed mental health professional, or other appropriate authority with any questions you may have regarding trauma, mental health, physical safety, medical conditions, or other professional matters.

By reading this book, you acknowledge and agree that neither the author nor the publisher shall be held liable for any injuries, losses, decisions, or outcomes, emotional, psychological, physical, relational, financial, or otherwise, that may arise directly or indirectly from the use or misuse of the content. The author and publisher expressly disclaim all warranties, express or implied, regarding the accuracy, applicability, or completeness of the information contained herein.

This book may reference sensitive topics, including trauma, abuse, mental health struggles, anxiety, depression, toxic relationships, emotional boundaries, and people-pleasing behaviors. Reader discretion is strongly advised. If you are experiencing acute distress, thoughts of self-harm, or feel unsafe, please contact a licensed professional immediately or reach out to emergency services in your country.

Some names, identifying details, and personal characteristics have been changed

ISBN: 978-1-969675-08-9 (paperback)

ISBN: 978-1-969675-09-6 (hardcover)

Scripture quotations are taken from various translations of the Bible as noted below:

TABLE OF CONTENTS

A NOTE FOR YOU, THE READER

Thank you for choosing this book. I know what it's like to carry a loud mind. To lie awake at night rehearsing fears, replaying regrets, or trying to control things already out of your hands. If you've felt that… I wrote this for you. And because peace isn't a one-time revelation, and because it's a practice, I created a free companion toolkit to walk with you beyond these pages.

You can download it here: **mikevestil.com/overthinking-gift**

(or scan the QR code below)

Inside, you'll find tools like:

1. **The Morning Stillness Reset:** A 5–10-minute daily ritual to quiet mental noise before it takes over. Includes breath guidance, Scripture, and grounding reflection to help you begin the day in peace instead of pressure.
2. **The Nighttime Release Ritual:** A calming, step-by-step evening practice to unload stress, release mental loops, and signal safety to your nervous system so you can rest deeply.

3. **The Overthinking Interruption Guide:** Short, practical prompts to use in the moment when your thoughts start spiraling. Designed to help you recognize fear-based thinking and gently replace it with truth.
4. **Fear to Faith Reflection Journal:** Ten guided journal prompts rooted in Scripture to help you uncover the fears driving your overthinking and reframe them through faith, compassion, and clarity.
5. **Relationship & Boundary Clarity Pages:** Gentle, honest questions to help you identify people-pleasing patterns, emotional overextension, and the moments you abandon yourself to keep the peace.
6. **Weekly Peace Check-In:** A simple one-page weekly reflection to track emotional patterns, notice growth, and reconnect with the calm you are learning to live from.

These are the tools I wish I had years ago when my thoughts felt louder than God and when my fear felt permanent. I hope these meet you in the moments you need them most.

With all my heart and hope,

Mike Vestil

INTRODUCTION

I THOUGHT I WAS LOSING MY MIND

3 a.m. My eyes snap open, and the race is already on. Anger is the first thing I feel. Anger at myself, at the clock, at the ceiling I'm about to study for the next two hours. Why can't I sleep? Why can't I just shut it off? I try to slow my breathing because a long day is waiting for me, and responsibility doesn't care how many hours I lost in the dark.

By morning, my partner looks rested, soft around the eyes, sunlight already kind to her face. I look wrecked. She asks how I slept. "Not good again, babe, but I've gotta get to work." Coffee. Keys. The drive I avoid thinking about because the place I'm heading isn't a calling; it's a stall. I can feel it in my bones. There's something out there bigger than the life I'm living now. Some kind of calling, some type of dream, or maybe it's a voice from God himself. And that voice? That voice is asking me to go after it. But here I am, showing up where I'm not respected by my colleagues who mistake volume for leadership.

At my desk, sleep ambushes me in the one place I can't surrender to it. My eyelids get heavy, and my head bobs. The drift pulls, and I fight it because the bills don't care, and the people I love are counting on me. How is it that the middle of the day makes me drowsy enough to slump in a chair, but night turns my mind into a siren?

Blink. The shift is over. Blink. I'm home. Blink. Dinner. My partner is talking, her mouth moving, and I want to be inside this moment, but I'm hovering two hours ahead, already bracing for the rematch with my thoughts. Blink. It's me in the bathroom mirror, anxious about the bed in the next room and the tiny little cracks in the ceiling that I'll count. Blink. Lights out. She's asleep in minutes. How does she do that? And here I am, pacing without moving.

The spiral starts. One thought bubble becomes ten. Financial responsibilities stretch taller than I remember. I see the faces of the people I love, a flicker of worry in their eyes because we're not where we need to be. My chest tightens, my legs tense, and I realize my jaw has locked itself without permission. I try to unclench. I try the tools from therapy. I try to name what's real and what isn't, what is objective vs. what is subjective. But my mind keeps changing the labels. Anxiety climbs my ribcage like ivy. Thoughts that don't sound like me start speaking with my voice. I handled panic in my twenties, but this older version is heavier, stickier, and crueler.

I tell myself not to check the clock. Damn it. I just checked the clock. I check again. And again. 4:02 a.m. The sun is somewhere in the hallway, waiting to walk in. I try to sprint toward sleep like it's a finish line I can break by force. My body begs for an off switch. An off switch with one button to press so I can drop into a deep, honest rest, the kind I haven't felt in forever. I feel how this is bleeding into everything: my relationships, my confidence, my focus, the way I show up for the people who think I'm strong. When did life get this hard? When did the mind become a room with no oxygen?

I've tried everything. I've tried talking it out with friends until I'm hoarse. I've tried therapy and the scripts the therapists make me practice. I've tried numbing myself with prescriptions and drinks that never keep their promises. Nothing quiets the voice that whispers the sentence I'm most afraid to hear: maybe I don't have what it takes to protect and provide. Maybe I can't create safety for a family if I can't even create safety in my own head. I picture a future where a child looks up at me and finds disappointment, not shelter, because their dad couldn't find a way to stand steady against invisible weather.

When a person runs out of options, the door they avoided starts to look like mercy. For me, that door was faith. I avoided it because of how it was handed to me. As a kid, drums and piano were forced love, and so I learned to resist what I was pushed to do. Church and prayer lived in that same drawer. They were guilt-stained and obligation-shaped.

I had prayed hard when I was young. It didn't stop the fights about money. It didn't stop the threats of my parents divorcing, or the slammed doors, or the belt that came out when my voice arrived at the wrong time. That kind of disappointment calcifies. So, I ran from the whole world of it.

But when nothing else worked, I decided to try again, not because I had answers but because I was out of them. I called a friend who lives close to God in a way that used to intimidate me. I didn't want a sermon. I didn't want someone to be "preachy" with me. And I didn't want someone else's guilt. I just wanted one concrete thing to do when the night turned loud. He gave me a simple line, almost embarrassingly simple: "When you feel it rising, say, 'I cast all of my burdens to the Christ within, and I go free.' Breathe. Then say it again."

I wanted to side-eye it. That's it? A sentence? But that night, when my partner slid into sleep and the ceiling started its show, I tried it. The spiral rose, I felt the money fear, the job fear, the future fear gathering like storm clouds, and I said it out loud, softly: *I cast all of my burdens to the Christ within, and I go free.* I inhaled like I hadn't all day. I exhaled like I was emptying a bag of rocks. The ivy loosened its grip a little. I said it again. *I cast all of my burdens to the Christ within, and I go free.* I noticed my glutes unclench, my legs stop bracing, and my shoulders slope down where they belong. I said it again. And again.

Blink. Morning. Somehow, the night passed without a fight. I didn't engineer it or analyze it into submission. I prayed, breathed, and let God be bigger than the noise. It wasn't magic; it was surrender. Prayer made a room in my mind where my heart could slow down, and when the heart slows, the mind listens.

That's when something clicked: my mind wasn't racing because it was broken; it was racing because my heart felt buried under a weight it was never meant to carry alone. In other seasons, I had tried releasing that weight to different names: the "universe" in faraway places with incense in the air or my parents when I was too young to understand what I was handing them. But all those trails led back to the same source. God. The more I practiced casting burdens to Christ, the more the night gave me back what it had stolen. The more rest I got, the more my days changed. My patience grew taller. My relationships softened. My health climbed out of the hole. Quiet returned to rooms where noise used to win.

Curiosity nudged me back to a book I'd kept at arm's length because of how it was wielded around me when I was young. The Bible had been a symbol of strict uncles and rigid rules in the Filipino houses where I learned to keep my head down. But with the shame stripped away, the pages felt different. I started with prayers that anchored me and verses that felt like handholds. Peace began to feel less like a rumor and more like muscle memory.

The funny thing is, millions of people have been preaching the power of God, faith, and prayer for thousands of years; yet for years, I didn't give it the time of day because of how boring I thought church was every Sunday, or how much I didn't like how my parents always forced me with guilt or shame to pray or that I was bad. So, I always turned away from it, trying to chase answers elsewhere, when little did I know, the secret to relieve my anxiety once and for all was hiding in plain sight my entire life.

And what I learned and experienced in those weeks after the crazy anxiety attacks and negative spirals, and the calm that began to settle in my mind when I fully surrendered to the short and simple prayers, journal prompts, and daily routines is what this book is built on: prayer isn't a performance; it's a habit that teaches the heart to release what it grips in fear. When the heart releases, the mind follows. When the mind quiets, a person can actually choose. They can choose presence over panic, truth over the lie that every thought is a command, rest over the theater of control.

Overthinking is a modern plague disguised as intelligence. But Scripture offers a deeper solution: not numbing, not avoidance, but renewal. This book is a blueprint to quiet the mind, strengthen the spirit, and reclaim peace in a world that profits from your anxiety. Read the prayers in this book in the sun before work, or whisper them at 3 a.m. when the ceiling starts talking again. Breathe with it. Walk with it. Sleep with it. Come with an open mind and a stubborn hope. I'm not promising a fix. I'm offering what has finally helped after trying everything else.

If a person is carrying anxiety alone, the loneliness makes the load feel heavier. I've found it helps to bring someone along: a friend, a spouse, a sibling who also knows what the midnight thought bubble attacks feel like. Not to fix each other. Just to walk the same path and share the same words when the air gets thin.

This is not a book about willpower. It's not an argument that a prayer replaces doctors, therapists, or the kind of help that keeps people grounded and safe. It's a companion for the moments between appointments and responsibilities, for the nights when shame talks too loud, for the mornings when work expects a fully formed person and all that shows up is a soul held together by a thread.

I still have nights where the old music tries to play. I still catch my jaw clenching, my legs bracing, and my thoughts sprinting toward worst-case cliffs. But I also have a sentence that fits in my pocket and a God who isn't bored of hearing it. *I cast all of my burdens to the Christ within, and I go free.* And somehow, one breath at a time, freedom walks in.

If this lands on the nightstand of someone who wakes up at 3 a.m. angry at a ceiling, I hope this book feels like a hand on a shoulder in the dark. If it sits at a kitchen table next to cold coffee after another rough night, I hope it feels like a chair pulled up by a friend who understands. This is the beginning. Turn the page. Let's practice peace until it sticks.

CHAPTER 1

STOP OVERTHINKING

It's approaching 8 p.m., and my anxiety is already rising. The past few days have felt like a quiet battle with my sanity and my sleep, and the exhaustion is starting to leak into everything. It's harder to communicate with my partner, harder to hold boundaries with people, and harder to focus on my work or my future. The lack of rest compounds it all.

Night after night, I lie awake staring at the ceiling, trying to control the spiral in my mind as thoughts loop and fears multiply. I toss and turn on the left side of the bed, careful not to wake my partner, while my body begs for rest that won't come. I think about how easily others seem to fall asleep, how natural it looks for them, while I negotiate with my thoughts and try to reason my way into peace. When did this become so hard? Sleep. The most natural thing in the world.

I talk to my therapist, the same one I've been seeing for weeks now, and I feel like I'm losing my mind. I've tried everything. Medication. Working out. Different supplements and drinks. Special pillows. Nothing sticks. So now, I talk about my feelings, even though I don't like doing that. I think it's because there's so much anger inside me, mostly aimed at myself. So much self-hatred. So much pity. A deep fear that I won't be able to provide for my family, that my worth as a man is fragile. I carry insecurities I've never fully named, shaped by growing up in a home where my parents slept in separate rooms and fighting felt normal.

I was hit as a child. I watched constant arguments and threats of divorce. No one noticed I was absorbing it all. I became the peacekeeper, the one who bent himself to keep the house from exploding. I became the mediator, the one sent to calm my father when he drank too much, the one told it was my responsibility to make things right. And guilt became my native language. I live inside it. Every decision feels soaked in it. Sometimes I wonder if that's why I can't sleep, because my mind never learned how to rest when it was trained to stay alert.

"Mike, so how do you feel?" the therapist asked.

"Fine," I said.

I didn't even realize how deep in my head I was until the session ended and I noticed I hadn't really heard a word my therapist said. I left and went home, feeling like nothing had shifted. My partner was there, making food, already settling into the evening, while I felt myself winding up again. The familiar pattern returned, me versus the spiral. I called the friend who once shared the prayer with me, the one that begins, *"I cast all my burdens to the Christ within, and I go free."* I asked him more about his faith, something I had pushed away for years after growing up under the weight of religious pressure and performance. I had learned to associate faith with obligation, not peace. But exhaustion has a way of humbling you. With the sleepless nights, the anxiety, and the constant mental noise, I was out of options. He shared his story, and this time, it landed differently. Pain has a way of opening doors that pride keeps shut. The same words I had heard before suddenly carried weight, as if suffering had tuned my ears to hear them for the first time.

Pain is weird. Pain is this emotion that opens your eyes. It's through suffering that you start to look at the world from a different perspective. And it's through that suffering that your mind really starts honing in and focusing on "synchronicities" or "coincidences" that just seem to happen.

For example, shortly after this talk with my friend, I went to visit my uncle. Well, he's not my uncle. He's my dad's best friend from when he was a kid living in the Philippines. He's a man who, at age 9, his father died, and by age 13, his mom essentially became a vegetable and couldn't think or support the family. So at an early age, he had to take the mantle as the leader of the household. I can't even imagine how he was able to do that at that age, when I'm struggling to do what he did, but as an adult. Why does it feel like I'm so behind? Why does it feel like no matter how hard I try to spin my wheels, I have this fear of financial scarcity that I won't be able to provide for my family?

Where does this come from? I know that it subconsciously comes from my mom and dad. The guilt I have for money, and my lack of deserving it, is apparent with all the times in the past I made money and lost money. I ended up meeting my uncle, who was able to crawl his way out of that situation and build multiple successful businesses in the hospitality industry, and I asked him what to do.

Now, normally, my uncle isn't really a man to talk about faith. He would always speak in a language that made sense to me: money and fun Chinese parables. It felt like I had my own little Mr. Miyagi. For as successful as he was, he dressed up like a homeless man wearing old T-shirts with stains on them.

I asked him, "Uncle, did you ever have a period where you felt like no matter how hard you pushed forward, you just couldn't get by?"

He answered, "Yes."

"What happened?"

"Years ago, I was in the middle of building up one of my hotels. Then, while building it, I was attacked by one of my competitors. Now, this was a difficult time because the kids were still small, and the competitors attacked me with politics, people inside the government who could control certain regulations, slandering my name in the media to the point where my wife and kids believed the news about their dad over their dad's words themselves. I was alone."

"How did you sleep?"

"I didn't."

"So, what did you do?"

"Normally, I would've wanted to attack him. I wanted to use the cash that I had left in the bank to fight the bastard that did this to me."

"Did you?"

"No."

"What did you do then?"

"I picked up the Bible and accidentally stumbled upon a parable that I needed to hear. When Moses was running away from the Egyptian army and had to choose between fighting the army or drowning in the Red Sea, he looked up at God and asked what to do. God replied, 'Do nothing, be still.'"

Exodus 14:14 reads, "The LORD will fight for you; you need only to be still."

"Be still. Be still?"

"Yeah, so I did nothing."

"Seriously?"

"Yes, and everything fixed itself, and I was able to heal my relationships with my family and kids, and the business boomed."

The more I looked deeper into this parable, I wanted to see how this plays with my overthinking. I think the Egyptian army is my thoughts, and the Red Sea is the to-do list of things that I think I need to do to get out of my negative thoughts. Maybe my need for control to fix my situation instead of being still and seeing where this situation brings me is the reason for my pain. Maybe my overthinking is a symptom of control addiction?

I researched more places in the Bible where this shows up:

Psalm 46:10, "Be still, and know that I am God." 1 Peter 5:7, "Cast all your anxieties on Him, because He cares for you."

Scripture doesn't shame anxiety; it invites us to release it. Overthinking is often mistaken for responsibility or intelligence, but spiritually, it's usually something else entirely. Overthinking is control dressed up as care. It's the belief that if I can just think hard enough, plan far enough ahead, or prepare for every outcome, I can keep myself safe. But faith doesn't ask for mastery. It asks for surrender.

Stillness is not passivity. It's not giving up or checking out. It's a quiet form of courage, a refusal to let fear dictate the next move. In a world that rewards constant motion and mental noise, stillness becomes a kind of rebellion. A decision to stop wrestling with the future and trust that you are being held, even when nothing is resolved yet.

That truth started to land for me when I visited my uncle. When he had the option to fight, he chose not to fight. Instead, he just stayed still. And slowly, things began to resolve themselves. His relationships healed. His business recovered. Peace returned.

As I sat with that story, something clicked. Maybe the army chasing me isn't external at all. Maybe it's my thoughts. My fear. My urgency to fix everything right now. Maybe the Red Sea is the future I keep trying to control instead of walking through with trust. Maybe my suffering isn't proof that I'm failing, but a signal that I'm gripping too tightly.

The Bible keeps returning to this theme. "Be still, and know that I am God." "Cast all your anxieties on Him, because He cares for you." Over and over, the message isn't to try harder, but to release more deeply.

Jesus once spoke of a seed that fell among thorns. The seed wasn't flawed. The soil wasn't barren. But the thorns that were worry, wealth, and the cares of life, slowly choked what was trying to grow. That's what overthinking does. It doesn't destroy you all at once. It suffocates you quietly. It fills every inch of space until there's no room left for peace to take root.

To receive peace, something has to be pulled out. Not punished. Not fought. Released. Stillness is not weakness. It is trust in motion. It is choosing to stop performing safety and allow God to be it. When I stopped trying to outrun my thoughts and instead laid them down, I felt something loosen. Not instantly. Not perfectly. But enough to breathe. Enough to sleep. Enough to believe that peace wasn't something I had to earn, only something I had to allow.

Modern Mindset vs. Biblical Wisdom

Modern Mindset	Biblical Wisdom
"Overthink every possible outcome"	"Be still, and know that I am God." (Psalm 46:10)
"Control = safety."	"Surrender = peace."
"Anxiety is a sign that I care."	"Anxiety is a burden to cast." (1 Peter 5:7)
"My value is based on how much I can predict."	"My value is rooted in being known and loved by God."
"Figure it all out before making a move."	"Take the next faithful step and trust God with the rest."
"If I stop thinking, everything will fall apart."	"If I stop striving, God steps in."
"Constant mental motion = growth."	"Inner stillness = spiritual depth."

I didn't fix my anxiety by forcing it to leave. What changed things was learning how to sit with it without trying to win. I started small:

five minutes in the morning or before bed. I'd sit down, place my hands open on my legs, and let myself stop performing. No solving. No optimizing. No trying to feel better. Just breathing and letting whatever noise was there pass through me. At first, it felt uncomfortable, almost unsafe, like I was doing something wrong by not trying to fix myself. But over time, my body began to understand that stillness wasn't danger. It was permission. Permission to rest without collapsing. Permission to exist without bracing for impact.

I also started writing things down. Not to analyze them, but to get them out of me. I would dump every worry onto the page, even the embarrassing ones, the ones that made me feel weak or ashamed. Then I would cross them out slowly, one by one. Not to deny they existed, but to release them. Something about physically striking through the words helped my body believe what my mind struggled to accept: I didn't have to carry everything at once. I wasn't meant to. That simple act became a way of telling myself, "You can set this down now."

Breathing became prayer before I even realized that's what it was. When the anxiety surged, I paired my breath with a quiet sentence. On the inhale, *Be still.* On the exhale, *and know that You are God.* I didn't force calm. I didn't chase peace. I just let the rhythm slow me down. It was subtle, but it worked. The breath gave my body something to hold onto when my thoughts wanted to run. Over time, those words began to feel less like something I was saying and more like something I was being held by.

Eventually, I anchored myself in one line of Scripture: *"Be still, and know that I am God."* I repeated it before sleep, when my mind started pacing, when the old fears crept in. It stopped feeling like a command and started feeling like an invitation. Not to fix myself.

Not to figure everything out. Just to rest inside something bigger than my fear. That's when I realized peace wasn't something I had to chase. It was something I could return to, again and again, as long as I was willing to stop fighting and let myself be held.

Journal Prompt: What thoughts have been looping in your mind lately? Write them down with no filters. Let them speak. Now, for each one ask: Is this true? Is this loving? Is this from God or from fear? What would it look like to release control and trust God with this thought?

CHAPTER 2

YOU ARE NOT YOUR THOUGHTS

"You're so stupid." The silence was unbearable.

I'm sitting in my beat-up, musty brown Honda Civic, the fabric on the ceiling held together with duct tape, parked in the middle of the lot at the gym where I used to work. I stare out over the dashboard in silence. That's when I first heard it: my "mind" speaking to me.

Usually, I'm rushing through the day, moving too fast to hear what's happening underneath the noise. It's like the low hum of an air conditioner or an old computer fan, always running in the background. You get so used to it that you stop noticing it's even there. That's what my mind was like. Quietly, constantly, it repeated the same message: *I am stupid.* I didn't realize how much that voice was shaping me. It shaped how I showed up with friends and family. It shaped how much I believed in myself when I tried to start something new. It shaped my fears about money, about failing, about not being able to provide for the people I love. That voice wasn't loud, but it was relentless, and it was steering far more of my life than I ever realized.

And I wondered why I walked around with slumped shoulders and no confidence, why I let people walk over me, why I was always people-pleasing and chasing validation from my partner or my parents. It was because this quiet voice in the back of my mind kept repeating the same message throughout the day. *I am stupid.* I didn't even notice it most of the time, but it shaped how I moved through the world, how small I made myself, and how much permission I gave others to define my worth.

So, there I was, sitting in my uncomfortable work uniform, instead of rushing to check off the next task like a good employee. For once, I didn't move. I didn't perform. I didn't chase the next thing my boss wanted from me. I just sat there and allowed myself to be still. And that's when I heard it clearly for the first time. A voice, loud and sharp, telling me how stupid I was. It startled me. Then a strange question followed right behind it.

Is this my voice? Do I actually believe this about myself? And if this voice isn't me, why does it sound exactly like me?

I sat there, turning the thought over in my mind, almost forgetting that I was about to be late for work. I kept wondering who this roommate in my head really was, and how long it had been living there without me noticing. I stared into the rearview mirror and saw a deep wrinkle forming between my eyebrows from how hard I was thinking. That was when it hit me that I was already late. I jumped out of the car and hurried toward the gym entrance. As I handed my card to the front desk to clock in, I felt my focus slipping again. That voice was still there, repeating, *I am stupid*, like a broken record. But now, it was quieter, almost sneaky, trying to fade into the background so I wouldn't notice it anymore. I realized that was how it usually worked. It hid just enough to run my thoughts, my emotions, and my reactions without being seen. That's how I spent most of my life, on autopilot, moving from one moment to the next, absorbing hits and reacting without awareness.

As I rushed toward the clock-in machine, I felt it trying to disappear again, retreating into some dark corner of my mind where it could pull the strings without being noticed. It felt like a small, twisted thing that thrived on my suffering. Right then, in the middle of the hallway, I stopped. I just stood there. People walked past me, throwing quick, uneasy glances as if I were strange or unstable. But I didn't care. I wanted to catch that little devil running away.

I grabbed that little voice in my mind with my thoughts and just looked at it kind of like how a flashlight is focused on a certain point in a dark room to illuminate it. That voice quivered in fear because now it was being seen and observed. It couldn't hide. But best of all, it couldn't manipulate me to do things that would have me create the same bad patterns. And as I kept looking at it, it started screaming louder as if it was being exorcised out of my mind.

Afraid that it had been caught, it started getting desperate. "I'm dumb, I'm an idiot, I will never succeed, I suck as a man," it screamed in terror as it tried to get under my skin. But something changed the moment I caught it and looked at it. I realized this thought was not me. Afraid that the cunning little thought devil was caught, it started shrieking even louder as the voice started getting deformed in my mind, no longer resembling my voice but that of a shrieking, dying little animal.

Desperate, that voice tried attacking me where I was weak. My relationship with my woman. The devil screamed, "My woman is ashamed that she settled for a man like me; she will probably leave me for someone better looking or more successful. She wakes up disappointed every single morning. My woman is not attracted to me. She wakes up disappointed that she sees me when she opens her eyes. She feels sorry for me. She regrets having met me. She's afraid that her family judges her for being with me when they know she can do better."

Normally, this would have gotten me. But the voice that was in my head. No longer resembled me. It was the first time that I could separate that voice from my true voice. And for the first time, I wasn't swayed by the voice, even when it came after my weakness and my need for validation from my woman, that it freaked out in terror as it slowly died in my mind, leaving nothing but space and stillness.

"Mike, you okay?" My coworker, who rushed past me, also late for work, saw me standing in the middle of the hallway and was curious as to why I suddenly stopped and stood there, blank-faced for the past minute.

"I've never been better," I responded.

And for the first time, it was true.

Not because my life had suddenly improved, but because something inside me had shifted. I had just watched a thought lose its power over me. For the first time, I saw that I could observe my mind without being swallowed by it. That moment stayed with me. It followed me home. It sat with me long after the adrenaline faded. And it slowly began to reframe everything I thought I knew about myself.

That was when a line from Scripture came back to me, one I had heard before but never really understood: *"We take every thought captive and make it obedient to Christ." – 2 Corinthians 10:5.*

I used to think that sounded extreme, even controlling. But now I realized it was describing something surprisingly gentle. It wasn't about suppressing thoughts or pretending they didn't exist. It was about recognizing that not every thought deserves authority. Not every thought is the truth. Some thoughts are just noise passing through a tired mind.

I began to see that thoughts behave like visitors. Some come with wisdom. Others come carrying fear, shame, or old wounds. And for most of my life, I had been treating every thought as if it were me. I believed them simply because they showed up. But Scripture was pointing to something different. It was saying that I have the ability to notice my thoughts without surrendering to them. To examine them. To choose which ones get to stay.

That idea alone was freeing. It meant the storm in my head wasn't my identity. It meant the chaos didn't define me. It meant I could pause, breathe, and ask, *Is this thought telling me the truth, or is it just loud?*

Another verse surfaced as I sat with this realization: *"Do not conform to the pattern of this world, but be transformed by the renewing of your mind." – Romans 12:2.* I used to think that meant becoming more disciplined or more religious. But now I see it differently. Renewal wasn't about trying harder. It was about seeing more clearly. It was about unlearning the stories I had absorbed about myself and letting something truer take their place.

The world trains us to live in reaction. To measure our worth by performance. To stay alert, anxious, and guarded. No wonder my mind felt like a battlefield. I had been living in survival mode for years, mistaking tension for responsibility and fear for wisdom. But the invitation here was different. It wasn't asking me to fight harder. It was asking me to come home to myself.

That's when the parable of the prodigal son took on new meaning for me. I had always heard it as a story about morality or redemption, but I missed the psychological depth of it. The son reaches a point where everything falls apart. He's broke, ashamed, and feeding pigs. And in that moment, he tells himself a story: *I am no longer worthy to be called a son.* That thought feels logical to him. It feels earned. It feels true. But it isn't.

When he returns home, the father doesn't argue with him. He doesn't list his mistakes. He doesn't make him earn his place back. He runs to him. He embraces him. He restores him. The father's response reveals something crucial. The son's identity was never lost, even when the son believed it was. The lie lived in the son's mind, not in the father's heart.

That realization landed hard for me. I had been living as if my worst thoughts were facts. As if my fear, my shame, and my self-criticism were accurate reflections of who I was. But what if they were just stories. I learned to tell myself? What if, like the prodigal, I had mistaken distance for disqualification?

I began to see that the voice in my head was not the voice of truth. It was the echo of old wounds, fears, and expectations that no longer served me. And the more I noticed it, the less power it had. Awareness didn't make it disappear overnight, but it loosened its grip. It reminded me that I was not broken. I was just listening to the wrong narrator.

That's what this chapter is really about. Not silencing your mind, but learning to listen differently. Not fighting your thoughts, but learning which ones deserve your trust. Because peace doesn't come from controlling every thought; it comes from realizing you don't have to believe them all.

And when that realization settles in, something soft opens inside you. You stop bracing. You stop performing. You stop trying to prove your worth. You remember that you were never meant to carry the weight of your identity alone. You were always meant to be held.

Modern Mindset vs. Biblical Wisdom

Modern Mindset	Biblical Wisdom
"Trust your thoughts."	"Take every thought captive." (2 Cor. 10:5)
"Follow your inner voice."	"My sheep hear My voice." (John 10:27)
"If I think it, it must be true."	"Test the spirits." (1 John 4:1)
"Shame is who I am."	"There is no condemnation." (Romans 8:1)
"Your thoughts define you."	"You are a new creation." (2 Cor. 5:17)
"Overthinking is responsible."	"Renew your mind daily." (Romans 12:2)
"Voice in my head = voice of truth."	"God's Word is the standard."

Once that truth settled in me, I realized something else: insight alone wasn't enough. Awareness opened the door, but I still had to learn how to live differently once I stepped through it. I couldn't just *know* that I wasn't my thoughts. I had to practice returning to that truth when my mind tried to drag me back into old patterns.

So, I started paying attention to the thoughts that showed up most often. The ones that repeated themselves like background noise. The ones that carried the most emotional weight. I began writing them down, not to analyze them, but to expose them. Seeing them on paper stripped them of their power. Thoughts like *I'm not enough*, *I'm behind*, *I'm a disappointment.*

Once they were written out, I asked a different question than I never had before. Instead of asking whether they felt true, I asked whether they were true. I held them up next to Scripture, not to shame myself, but to see the contrast. And almost every time, the difference was obvious. What I believed about myself was harsh, condemning, and final. What God spoke was steady, patient, and full of invitation. Writing the truth beside the lie didn't magically erase the lie, but it loosened its grip. It reminded me that my thoughts were not the authority. Truth was.

I also started paying attention to how I spoke to myself. I realized that most of my inner dialogue sounded nothing like love. It sounded like an accusation. So, I began practicing something that felt awkward at first. I started speaking identity out loud. Simple things. "I am loved." "I am not abandoned." "I am learning." "I am held." On the days when it felt fake, I said them anyway. Not as affirmations to convince myself, but as declarations to remind myself who I belonged to. I wasn't trying to hype myself up. I was trying to realign with something truer than my mood.

Over time, I learned to pause when a thought hit hard. Instead of immediately believing it, I asked a simple question: *Whose voice is this?* And then a second one: *Would God speak to me this way?* That question alone changed everything. Shame always demanded urgency. Love never did. Condemnation rushed me. Grace waited. When I learned to tell the difference, the volume of the lies dropped. They didn't disappear, but they lost their authority.

And then there was the practice that helped out a lot. When shame showed up, I stopped trying to outrun it or reason it away. I pictured myself turning toward God instead of away. Not as a fearful child bracing for punishment, but as someone being welcomed home. I imagined Him moving toward me, not disappointed, not annoyed, but glad I had come back. That image softened something deep inside me. It rewired the instinct to hide. Over time, I stopped running from the feeling and started letting it lead me back to safety.

That's when I understood what it really meant to be held. Not fixed. Not corrected. *Held.* These practices didn't make me perfect or immune to fear. But they gave me a way to return to myself when I drifted. They gave me a way to listen without obeying every thought. And slowly they taught me that the voice of love had been there all along, waiting for me to stop running long enough to hear it.

Journal Prompt: Write down 3 thoughts you've had in the past 48 hours that made you feel small, ashamed, or stuck.

For each one, ask: Where did this thought come from? Is this what God would say to His child? What truth can I speak back to it?

CHAPTER 3

LET GOD BE GOD

I've stood at so many forks in the road that I've lost count. Should I choose dentistry, or should I follow my calling? Should I make decisions based on my parents' wishes, or finally choose for myself instead of living with guilt? Should I stay in this relationship because it's familiar, even if it's slowly draining me, or should I walk away and face the discomfort of being alone again? Should I start a family now, or wait until I feel more financially secure? Should I keep living in the place I grew up, or leave and explore the world, maybe even build a life somewhere new?

These questions used to loop endlessly in my mind. Night after night, I would toss and turn, trying to escape them just long enough to get a few hours of rest. All I wanted was to sleep deeply, to shut my mind off for once, to experience a night without thinking myself in circles. But the thoughts wouldn't let me go. They followed me into the dark, demanding answers I didn't yet have.

I started to notice that most of my thoughts were tied to two things: money and relationships. As I continued shining the flashlight on the ruins left behind by that "devil voice" I had just driven out through stillness and observation, a pattern became clear. Those two areas were where most of my anxiety lived. Nearly every fear, every spiral, every moment of self-doubt seemed to trace back to them.

Whenever one of those two areas fell out of balance, the "devil voice" would grow louder. It would start pulling me in every direction, guiding my reactions and decisions without me even realizing it. I wasn't choosing anymore. I was reacting. A lot of the choices I made came from unresolved dynamics with my mom and dad. Their expectations, their approval, their disappointment still lived inside me, quietly shaping my behavior long after I thought I had outgrown it.

I love my mom and dad deeply. Today, they are some of my closest friends, and I speak often about the beautiful memories we've created as they've grown older and softer with time. But growing up, it wasn't always like that. When I was a child, discipline often came in the form of fear. Being smacked or hit with a belt was normal. When I misbehaved, my dad would lock me in a room, and I would scream to be let out, eventually crying myself quiet because there was nothing else I could do. I learned early how to survive by shrinking, by staying still, by waiting for the storm to pass.

We also had an extended grandparent living with us, a relative of my grandmother who stayed in our home for a long time. Every day, without exception, I was made to take a nap at 11 a.m. Not encouraged or guided. Forced. If I didn't sleep, I was punished. Sometimes, that meant being hit with a belt across my back. Other times, that meant being slapped across the face until I behaved. Rest wasn't something I learned to associate with safety or care. It was something enforced through fear.

Because I was the only Asian kid at my school, I stood out in ways I didn't know how to protect myself from. I was chased by bigger kids, pushed around, and called names because I looked different. I didn't have the words for it then, but I learned early what it felt like to be singled out, to be seen as other, and to carry shame for something I couldn't change.

My parents were so busy trying to survive that they didn't see what was happening. They were dealing with their own weight, their own fears. They had moved from the Philippines to America with almost nothing, raising two kids they could barely afford, carrying responsibilities that never seemed to lighten. Their relationship wasn't built on ease or romance, but on duty and endurance. Love existed, but it was buried under stress, exhaustion, and the constant pressure to keep going. Looking back, I don't blame them. They were doing the best they could with what they had.

My mom carried a lot of disappointment early in her marriage. My dad had lost everything right before they got married, and the financial weight fell almost entirely on her shoulders. While he went door to door selling newspapers, chasing small side hustles, and trying to find his footing while studying engineering, she carried the pressure of keeping the household afloat. It wasn't that he wasn't trying. It was that the uncertainty never seemed to end, and the strain settled quietly between them.

Growing up in that environment, a belief slowly took root in me. If I didn't have money, my family wouldn't be safe. If I didn't have money, I wouldn't be worthy of love. If I didn't have money, my wife would regret choosing me. If I didn't have money, my children would suffer. If I didn't have money, I would fail as a man.

Money became more than currency. It became protection. Identity. Proof of worth. Somewhere along the way, it stopped being a tool and turned into a measure of my value as a human being.

Money. Money. Money.

The "devil voice" in my mind would whisper, *"My precious. My precious."* Somewhere along the way, I had turned money into a god. A god I served without realizing it. A god that dictated my choices, shaped my identity, and quietly fed my insecurities. Money became the measure of my safety, my worth, and my future. And without noticing it at first, I built my entire sense of stability around it. What I didn't see then was that this false god was also the root of my anxiety, my stress, and the endless mental spirals that kept me trapped.

I would think, *Maybe I should chase this new path. It feels more aligned. It feels alive.* And then the other voice would creep in. *But money,* it would whisper. The little devil, rubbing its hands together like a mosquito circling skin, waiting for the right moment to feed. It watched me with that familiar, impish grin, reminding me of all the reasons I shouldn't move, shouldn't risk, shouldn't trust myself.

As I got older, other desires started entering my mind. *Maybe it's time to start a family. Maybe it's time to build something real.* And then the devilish imp would appear again. *But money,* it would whisper, rubbing its little hands together with a crooked grin. It would remind me of every fear I carried about not being enough. It would tell me her parents looked down on me, that they saw me as a disappointment, someone she had settled for. It hissed that they judged her for choosing me, that they believed she could have done better. The imp laughed quietly as it fed on my doubt, whispering that I would never measure up, that love without money was foolish, and that I would always fall short.

And because money had become my measuring stick, dentistry became the answer. I chose it not out of passion, but out of fear. I took all my dreams of travel, adventure, laughter, and a life filled with shared moments and tucked them away. I placed them in a box and pushed it into the far corner of my mind. I scribbled a label across it that read, *"Dreams aren't worth it."* Then I left it there to collect dust in the darkest part of me, untouched for years.

But God seemed to have a different plan for me. Looking back, I think He always knew that path wasn't truly mine. For some people, it might be. But for me, I believe He had something bigger in mind. And I think He grew frustrated watching me ignore it. Not in anger, but in that quiet, patient way only God can have when He knows someone is walking away from what they were made for.

I started to imagine that God has a kind of knob connected directly to our hearts. When He sees us drifting toward something that will slowly hollow us out, He turns it just a little. Not to punish us, but to get our attention. The problem is that we move so fast through life that we rarely sit still long enough to notice. We fill every silence, chase every obligation, distract ourselves from discomfort. And in doing so, we drown out His voice.

I was living in constant reaction. The devilish imp inside me would tug on my strings, and I would move without thinking, like a puppet. Whenever I lived in reaction instead of stillness, I lost the ability to hear the true voice inside me. The voice that didn't shout or shame. The voice that carried clarity. The voice that was aligned with God's own.

So, God kept turning the knob. A little more pressure. A little more discomfort. Not to hurt me, but to wake me up. I began to believe that anxiety wasn't a punishment at all, but a signal. A signal that I was moving too fast, too far, and too disconnected from what mattered. It was His way of saying, *Slow down. Pay attention. You're going the wrong way.*

I imagine Him watching me from above, shaking His head as I sprinted in the wrong direction, ignoring every sign along the path. Finally, He reached for the emergency lever, the one marked *"Use only when he refuses to listen."* And He turned it. Not out of cruelty, but out of care. Not to break me, but to bring me back.

When I began to see anxiety that way, everything changed. It stopped feeling like an enemy and started to feel like an invitation. An uncomfortable one, yes. But also, a loving one. A call to slow down, to listen, and to return to the path I had wandered from.

For example, as dental school got closer, my anxiety began to rise. At first, it was subtle, like a low hum in the background. But as the start date approached, it grew louder and heavier. It felt like God was slowly turning a dial. A little at first. Then more. And more.

I would lie awake at night staring at the ceiling, asking myself why I couldn't sleep. *I need to go to bed. I have responsibilities tomorrow,* I would tell myself, bargaining with my own mind. But the quieter the world became, the louder everything inside me grew. Those late hours felt different. Heavy. Almost intentional. I started to wonder if the anxiety was anxiety at all. Maybe it was God knocking, saying, *I kept you awake because this is the only time you're quiet enough to hear Me.*

Looking back, I think God grew tired of waiting for me to notice. I think He turned the dial even further. My anxiety climbed to a ten out of ten. My girlfriend at the time cheated on me. The friends I leaned on disappeared. The distractions that once kept me comfortable were stripped away one by one. I was left alone, standing at one of the biggest crossroads of my life, facing decisions that would shape the next forty years. It felt brutal. It felt unfair. But it also felt intentional.

And then, something strange started to happen. In the middle of all that pain, God began placing things in my path with eerie precision. A personal development coach I had followed for years suddenly appeared in my small Midwestern town. Books I needed seemed to fall into my hands at exactly the right moment. Conversations happened that felt too perfectly timed to be a coincidence. It was as if anxiety, loss, and disruption were being mixed with purpose.

That's when I started to notice a pattern. God seems to use pain as a doorway. He pairs discomfort with invitation. He allows pressure to build until we finally slow down enough to listen. Sometimes that invitation comes through a stranger. Sometimes through heartbreak. Sometimes through loss. Sometimes, through a quiet moment, that changes everything.

And still, in the middle of it, I remember asking, *Why, God? Why are you doing this to me? Why does my life feel so full of pain right now?* I couldn't see the bigger picture. I couldn't understand why everything felt like it was falling apart. But maybe that was the point. Maybe I didn't need to understand the whole plan. Maybe I just needed to stop running long enough to let Him work.

Isn't it strange how God works like that sometimes? How He uses discomfort to guide us, and confusion to wake us up? How He places us in moments so uncomfortable that all we can do is listen? I'm starting to believe that sometimes the pain isn't punishment at all. Sometimes, it's an invitation. An invitation to be still, to trust, and to wait for the next small miracle that He quietly places in front of us, right in the middle of the most painful season of our lives.

As I sat with all of this, something else began to take shape in me. A realization I couldn't unsee once it surfaced. I started to notice that so much of my overthinking wasn't wisdom at all. It was fear wearing the costume of responsibility. It was anxiety pretending to be preparation. I had always believed that thinking more meant caring more, that planning meant protecting myself and the people I loved. But slowly, and painfully, I began to see that most of my overthinking wasn't rooted in trust. It was rooted in control.

There's a verse in the Bible that says, *"Trust in the Lord with all your heart, and lean not on your own understanding." – Proverbs 3:5.* For most of my life, I thought that meant ignoring logic or suppressing thought. But I see now that it means something much deeper. It means recognizing the limits of my own mind. It means understanding that my need to overanalyze every outcome isn't wisdom, it's fear trying to feel safe.

When anxiety shows up, my instinct is to plan harder. To think further ahead. To map out every possible future so nothing can surprise me. More spreadsheets. More scenarios. More backup plans. But God never asked me to trust my planning. He asked me to trust Him. And that difference is everything.

Because when I'm honest with myself, the root of my overthinking isn't intelligence. It's the quiet belief that if I loosen my grip, everything will fall apart. That I am the one holding the world together. That if I stop managing, predicting, and controlling, something terrible will happen. That belief sounds responsible on the surface, but underneath it is fear. And fear, no matter how sophisticated, is still fear.

The kingdom God invites us into doesn't run on fear. It runs on trust. Faith isn't pretending things are fine or ignoring reality. Faith is choosing to step forward even when the path isn't fully lit, because you trust the One guiding you. It's not about certainty. It's about a relationship.

That's why the story of Peter walking on water suddenly made sense to me in a way it never had before. When Peter saw Jesus walking on the sea, he asked to come, too. And Jesus didn't lecture him. He didn't give him a plan or a safety net. He simply said, *"Come."* And Peter stepped out of the boat. For a moment, impossibly, he walked on water. Not because the storm stopped, but because his focus was fixed.

But the moment Peter looked at the wind, everything changed. The waves didn't suddenly get stronger. The storm didn't become more dangerous. What changed was where his attention went. He shifted from trust to fear. From presence to prediction. And that's when he began to sink.

That story felt uncomfortably familiar. I wasn't sinking because life was too hard. I was sinking because I kept taking my eyes off what was holding me. My anxiety didn't come from the storm. It came from my fixation on it.

That realization softened something in me. I began to understand that faith isn't the absence of fear. It's the choice to move forward even when fear is loud. It's choosing trust when control feels safer.

It's learning to walk without needing to see the whole path at once.

And maybe that's what all of this has been teaching me. That the moments I thought were breaking me were actually invitations. Invitations to loosen my grip. To stop white-knuckling my future. To trust that, even when I can't see the next step, I am not walking alone.

Maybe I don't need to understand everything to move forward. Maybe I just need to take the next step, listen for the quiet guidance beneath the noise, and trust that the One who called me here knows the way ahead better than I ever could.

Modern Mindset vs. Biblical Wisdom

Modern Mindset	Biblical Wisdom
"Control every outcome before acting."	"Walk by faith, not by sight." (2 Cor. 5:7)
"Make sure it makes sense first."	"Lean not on your own understanding." (Prov. 3:5)
"If you don't know every step, don't move."	"Your word is a lamp to my feet." (Psalm 119:105)
"You are the architect of your future."	"You are the clay. He is the potter." (Isaiah 64:8)
"Anxiety is being smart."	"Anxiety weighs the heart, but a kind word cheers it up." (Prov. 12:25)
"Faith is reckless."	"Without faith it is impossible to please God." (Hebrews 11:6)
"You need full clarity before obedience."	"Abraham obeyed... not knowing where he was going." (Heb. 11:8)

Once I began to hear that voice again, I realized something else. Peace didn't come from solving my life. It came from learning how to stop fighting it. I didn't need a new personality or a perfectly mapped plan. I needed practices that helped me remember who was actually in control. I needed small, daily ways to step out of my own grip and back into trust.

The first thing that changed was my mornings. I noticed how quickly I reached for my phone, how instinctively I wanted to check messages, news, and notifications, anything that would pull me into reaction before I was even awake. So, I stopped. Before touching anything, I started whispering a simple prayer while my eyes were still heavy: *God, I release my need to control today. Lead me. I'll follow.* Some mornings, I meant it. Other mornings, I didn't. But I said it anyway. And slowly, it began to soften something in me. It reminded me that the day didn't belong to my anxiety. It didn't belong to my plans. It belonged to God.

I also began creating space where nothing was allowed to speak to me except my own breath and whatever God wanted to surface. No phone. No music. No podcasts. No planning. Just silence. At first, it was uncomfortable, almost unbearable. My mind would scramble for stimulation, for something to grab onto. But eventually the noise thinned out. And underneath it, there was a quieter voice. Not demanding. Not anxious. Just steady. I started to realize how much of my fear had been fueled by constant input. When I removed the noise, God didn't have to shout anymore.

Then I changed the way I made decisions. Instead of rushing or obsessing, I began placing them in front of God like offerings. I would write them down and ask a simple question: *Am I leading this, or am I being led?* I wasn't asking for a sign or a miracle. I was asking for alignment. There was a difference. Some choices immediately felt heavy and tight. Others felt calm, even if they were uncertain. I learned to trust that feeling. Not because it was comfortable, but because it carried peace instead of panic.

And when I felt overwhelmed, when my mind wanted to run ten steps ahead, I practiced narrowing my focus. I stopped asking myself how everything would work out and started asking what the next right step was. Just one. Not the whole staircase. Not the entire future. Just the next faithful movement forward. That alone was enough to quiet the noise.

Little by little, these practices rewired something in me. They didn't make life easy, but they made it honest. I stopped trying to control outcomes and started learning how to listen. And in that listening, I found something I had been chasing for years without realizing it wasn't something to chase at all. It was something to receive.

Journal Prompt: Write down a big decision you're facing. Now ask honestly: Where am I grasping for control instead of surrender? What outcome am I afraid to release? What would it look like to trust God even if the next step is unclear?

CHAPTER 4

RETURN TO THE PRESENT

The lake looks beautiful today, I think to myself as I sit on the roof of this tiny little lake boat in the middle of Lake Geneva, a small lake town in the Midwest. It's the first week of summer vacation, and it feels good to finally be out of school. Free from the stress of wearing a mask just to fit in. Free from worrying about getting made fun of for being shy, skinny, or weird. At least here, on this lake, I feel safe. I'm surrounded by my family and extended family as we get ready to celebrate my mom's birthday.

But my mind is already starting to race.

I think this might be the moment when the weight of the future first began pressing on my chest. It's strange how it happens. One moment, you're just a kid. You're born without knowing who or what you are. Then suddenly you're aware. I remember flashes: a man making funny noises at me, trying to get my attention with some beeping toy. A woman smiling, shaking something in front of my face. "Look at your dad," she says. "Smile, baby, goo goo." Mom. Dad. Somehow, I know these people belong to me.

Then another blink. There's a small bundle in my mom's arms.

"Take care of her; she's your little sister," she says. Another blink. I'm sitting in elementary school, drinking chocolate milk in silence, while a kid yells, "Why do your eyes look like that?" Another blink. I'm thirteen, sitting in front of a counsellor who tells me, "Now you have to decide what you want to do with the rest of your life. The choices you make now will determine whether you succeed or fail."

And now, I'm here. Sitting on this boat. Feeling the weight of all of it land at once. The future. The expectations. The pressure to choose correctly. To not mess it up. To become someone worthy of love, safety, and respect. I think this is when the spirals really started. The moment I realized that life wasn't just happening to me anymore. It was waiting for me to decide who I was going to be.

It's strange, really. Life feels like one long string of moments where you blink, and suddenly, you're in a different body, in a different place, in a different version of your life. New homes. New environments. Parents who seem to age faster than you're ready for. And then, before you even understand who you are, the world starts demanding answers from you. Big ones.

Decide now, it says. *Choose your future. Choose correctly, or you'll fail forever.* All of that pressure lands long before you've had the chance to understand yourself, your values, or the kind of life you actually want to build.

Reaction. Reaction. Reaction.

Like a wounded animal, shocked in one direction, running the other way only to get shocked again. I felt like I was bouncing through life blind, ricocheting between moments of pain, confusion, and fear. And then years pass, and one day, you wake up carrying a quiet resentment toward yourself, without fully knowing how it got there.

That was my inner world growing up. Those were the thoughts forming as my awareness slowly woke up during my teenage years. And as I sat there on that boat, my mind racing, I couldn't help but notice the kids of my mom's coworkers laughing nearby. I watched them while we drifted on that rickety, sun-bleached boat we'd rented for two hours. I noticed my dad sitting there, too, his eyebrows scrunched together, probably calculating how much this day had cost us. The gas for the long drive. The rental. The food. All of it, weighing on him silently.

We had driven four hours from our small, beat-up duplex just to be there. And in that moment, surrounded by water, laughter, and noise, I felt the pressure of it all pressing in. The money. The expectations. The unspoken fear of not measuring up. That was the backdrop of my childhood. That was the soil my thoughts grew in.

My future? My future? I have to decide what I'm going to do for the rest of my life at thirteen years old? Are you kidding me? Why does society put so much pressure on a kid? *I'm only thirteen. Can't they give me a break?*

"You have no choice, son. That's life," my dad would say as he got ready for another long day of work. "You work, then you die."

I look up at the sky. Birds glide effortlessly above the lake. The sky feels wide and endless here, and for a moment, I wish I could be like them. Free. Unburdened. But I'm not. My mind is racing faster and faster, thoughts barking at me that I'm already falling behind, that I'm going to make the wrong decision, that I'm already messing up my future at thirteen years old. It feels like the devilish imp had already found its way into my head back then, whispering doubt before I even knew what doubt was.

And then it hits me. A thought flashes through my mind: *Do a backflip. Get their attention. Make them look at you.* Maybe then, I'll feel seen. Maybe then, I'll feel like I belong.

Before I can overthink it, I climb onto the roof and attempt my first-ever backflip, desperate for approval, for validation, for something that tells me I matter.

I jump backward and curl into a ball. The world flips, and suddenly everything is spinning as the dark blue water swallows my small body.

Silence.

I'm deep under the surface. The world goes quiet. For a moment, everything stops. The noise in my head disappears. There is no fear, no pressure, no thoughts at all. Just stillness. Peace. If only I could stay here forever. Then a voice cuts through the calm. "You need air." It sounds like me. "Swim up." I panic. I don't know which way is up or down. My arms start flailing wildly, like a butterfly trapped in water, desperate to find the surface. I break through with a gasp. Air floods my lungs. I'm alive.

But then I look around.

Where is the boat?

My heart drops. It's far away. Too far. The angle I came up at pushed me even farther than I realized. I start dog-paddling toward it, fear creeping in. My thoughts spiral instantly. *You can't swim. You're weak. You're going to drown.*

I try to calm myself, but my body betrays me. All those swimming lessons my mom forced me into never really stuck. I was a skinny kid, barely any muscle, barely any fat to help me float. My lungs were weak, and asthma always tightened my chest when I panicked. I was never built for this. My arms start to burn. The boat still looks so far away.

"You can't make it," the devilish imp whispers. And I believe him.

"Help!" I scream.

My family looks over and laughs, thinking I'm joking. My panic spikes. The imp laughs, too, delighted. "I told you," it sneers. "Look how weak you are."

I flail harder, wasting what little strength I have left. My arms feel like lead. My chest burns. My mom finally realizes something is wrong. She starts yelling, throwing life jackets toward me. But she's panicking and none of the jackets reach me. The wind keeps pushing the boat farther away. Each life jacket hits the water just out of reach, mocking me.

And there I am, exhausted, terrified, and sinking, while the world keeps moving like nothing is wrong. I see my dad panic. He hates the sun. He had just gotten a new job and was given an expensive work phone. He had been standing in the corner of the boat, taking calls, when he suddenly realized I was drowning. Without thinking, he jumped in after me, forgetting the phone was still in his pocket as he hit the water.

I love you, Dad, I think as he swims toward me.

All I can see is his long-sleeve shirt and his hair, already starting to gray from the stress of work. I'm swallowing water now, and my vision flickers. Sometimes, I see the sky. Sometimes, everything goes dark. I can't tell which way is up anymore. My body keeps trying to breathe, even though there's nothing but water.

He reaches me and grabs hold, trying to swim us both back. He doesn't realize how hard it is to swim while holding a panicking child. Or maybe it's because he was heavier then, worn down by stress and drinking. His arm wraps around my neck as he breaststrokes with the other, and I start choking. I swallow more water. My lungs burn. It feels like there's more water inside me than air.

Now he's panicking too. I can feel it. The boat is farther away than it looks. My mind starts spiraling again. *You're going to kill him.*

The devilish imp laughs inside my head. "You're the reason your dad is going to die."

Guilt crashes over me. A heavy, suffocating weight. I hear my mom screaming from the boat, but her voice sounds distant, like it's coming from another world. I can barely make out the sound. I start to think this is it.

I gather whatever strength I have left and push upward, trying to lift my dad so he can breathe. I sink beneath him, swallowing more water, my chest burning. Everything feels slow now. Heavy. Fading.

How long has this been happening? I wonder. I'm so tired. Thirteen years old. Blink. Dead. What a life. I give up.

I start seeing the light. And for some reason, I feel calm. Completely calm. In that moment, everything else disappears. I forget about tomorrow. I forget about the future I've been so afraid of. I forget about the career my counselor said I had to choose. I forget my parents fighting. I forget my dad's drinking. I forget the fear of ending up alone. I forget the fear of money, of failure, of not being enough. I forget the pressure of what everyone else expects from me.

I forget everything.

Because at this moment, I think I'm going to die. And suddenly, none of it matters. Not even a little. A hand grabs me.

It's small. Too small. I feel confused. Whose hand is this? Why is it so light?

Then I'm being pulled upward. I gasp for air. I'm floating. Why am I floating? How is this happening? I cling to something soft and buoyant, something that feels like a pillow lifting me out of the water. My breathing slows. My body starts to calm.

Then I see her.

It's my little sister, Angelique. She's four years younger than me. Tiny. Fragile. Wearing a life jacket, somehow holding onto my dad and me at the same time, keeping us afloat.

That's when I understood why my parents named her Angelique. Because that day, she was an angel. If it weren't for her, my dad and I wouldn't have made it.

As we drift back toward the boat, I see my dad's face. Pale. Drained. His eyes wide with fear. We're both exhausted, barely holding ourselves together. The boat driver finally reaches us and pulls us in. I cough violently, throwing up water and half-digested food. My dad collapses beside me. My mom is crying. My sister sits there quietly, still holding onto her life jacket.

We're alive.

In that moment, something breaks open inside me. I realize how little the future actually matters when you're face-to-face with death.

All the stress, all the planning, all the anxiety about who I'm supposed to become fades into nothing. Tomorrow isn't promised. Control is an illusion.

That moment taught me something my mind would spend years trying to relearn. When you're that close to the edge, the only thing that exists is now. Presence. Breath. Being alive.

And somehow, in the middle of fear, I found peace.

As I lay there afterward, soaked and shaking, something inside me began to shift. Not all at once. Not like a lightning bolt. More like a quiet settling. A realization that crept in slowly, almost shyly, as my breathing returned to normal and my body remembered it was still alive.

I kept thinking about how close I had come to dying. How easily everything I worried about could have disappeared in an instant. All the planning. All the fear. All the pressure I put on myself to figure out my entire future before I was even old enough to understand who I was. None of it mattered in that moment. None of it followed me into the water.

What stayed was breath. Presence. The simple fact that I was still here.

That's when I began to understand something I wouldn't have words for until much later in life. That most of my suffering didn't come from what was actually happening, but from where my mind kept running. I was always living ahead of myself. Tomorrow. Next year. Ten years from now. What if I fail? What if I disappoint everyone? What if I end up alone? My mind lived everywhere except where my body was standing.

Years later, I would read a line that stopped me cold: *"Do not worry about tomorrow, for tomorrow will worry about itself." – Matthew 6:34.* It sounded almost too simple. Almost dismissive. But the more I sat with it, the more I realized it wasn't minimizing pain. It was redirecting attention. It wasn't saying tomorrow doesn't matter. It was saying tomorrow isn't yours to carry today.

I began to see that God never promised to give me strength for my entire future. He promised something much quieter, much smaller, and somehow much more powerful. *"Give us this day our daily bread." – Matthew 6:11.* Not weekly bread. Not five-year plans. Just today.

That idea unsettled me at first. I wanted guarantees. I wanted certainty. I wanted to know that everything would work out before I took a step. But grace, I was learning, doesn't work that way. Grace shows up in the moment you're standing in, not the ones you're rehearsing in your head.

I started to notice how often my anxiety lived in imaginary futures. Futures that hadn't happened. Futures that might never happen. Futures my mind invented and then punished me for. And yet, right here, in this moment, I was breathing. I was alive. I was okay.

That's when I remembered the story of the Israelites wandering in the desert. God gave them manna to eat, but only enough for one day. If they tried to hoard it, it spoiled. It rotted overnight. At first, that always confused me. Why wouldn't God want them to feel secure? Why not give them a week's worth? Or a month's worth?

But now I think I understand. The manna wasn't just food. It was training. It was teaching them how to trust, teaching them how to wake up each day and depend, not on what they had stored, but on what would be given. It taught them presence. Dependence. Faith.

And maybe that's what I had been missing all along.

I kept trying to store up certainty for a future that didn't exist yet. I wanted guarantees before I moved. Assurance before I trusted. Proof before I rested. But faith doesn't work like that. Faith asks you to stand where you are and trust that tomorrow's grace will show up when tomorrow arrives.

I started to see that my anxiety and overthinking weren't signs that I was broken. They were signs that I was trying to live in a time that wasn't mine yet. That I was carrying tomorrow's weight with today's strength. And no one is built to carry that.

Grace, I realized, is not something you stockpile. It's something you receive, moment by moment. Breath by breath. Day by day.

And maybe that's why, in that water, when I thought I was about to die, everything became clear. Because I wasn't living in tomorrow anymore. I was just here. Breathing. Existing. Alive. And somehow, that was enough.

Modern Mindset vs. Biblical Wisdom

Modern Mindset	Biblical Wisdom
"Plan the next 5 years perfectly."	"Trust God daily." (Matthew 6:11)
"Obsess over long-term security."	"Each day has enough trouble of its own." (Matthew 6:34)
"Visualize your dream life	"Delight in the Lord, and He

constantly."	will give you the desires of your heart." (Psalm 37:4)
"Grind now so you can enjoy later."	"Sabbath was made for man." (Mark 2:27)
"Delay joy until success."	"This is the day the Lord has made." (Psalm 118:24)
"Worry about everything you can't control."	"Cast your cares on Him." (1 Peter 5:7)
"The present is a means to the future."	"The present is where God dwells."

After that day, I started to notice something. Peace didn't come from fixing my life. It came from landing in it, from being where my feet were instead of where my fears kept dragging me. I didn't figure this out all at once. It came slowly, through small experiments, small moments where I chose presence over panic.

Mornings were the first place it began to change. I used to wake up already behind, already anxious, already mentally racing through everything I had to do. My mind would sprint ahead before my body even left the bed. So, one morning, before checking my phone, before moving at all, I whispered something simple: *God, I receive the grace for today. Not tomorrow.* It felt awkward at first. Almost too small to matter. But something shifted when I said it. It reminded me that I didn't need strength for a lifetime. I just needed enough for the next few hours. And somehow, that was always there.

I also began to notice how uncomfortable I was with rest. Real rest. Not collapsing from exhaustion, but choosing to stop. I realized I treated stillness like laziness and rest like weakness. So, I started carving out time where I didn't produce anything at all. No work.

No productivity. No improvement. Sometimes it was an hour. Sometimes it was a full day. I'd sit, walk, listen, or just exist. At first, guilt screamed at me. But slowly, something softened. I started to feel that rest wasn't me falling behind. It was me trusting that the world didn't need my constant effort to keep spinning.

At night, I began asking myself a different kind of question. Not *What did I accomplish?* or *What did I mess up?* but *What was one sacred moment I almost missed today?* Sometimes, it was small. The way sunlight hits the floor. A laugh I didn't expect. A moment of quiet when my mind didn't race. Noticing those moments taught me something important: presence doesn't arrive with fireworks. It shows up quietly and waits to be noticed.

And when my thoughts started spiraling again, as they often did, I learned to interrupt them gently, not with force, but with grounding. I would name five things I could see. A sound. A texture. A color. Something I was grateful for right then. Not yesterday. Not someday. Right now. It pulled me out of the future and back into my body, back into the moment where life was actually happening.

Over time, I realized these weren't techniques. They were acts of trust. Each one was a way of saying, *I don't need to carry tomorrow yet.* Each one was a quiet agreement with God that this moment, right here, was enough to hold me.

And slowly, without me forcing it, peace began to return. Not all at once. Not permanently. But often enough that I could feel it again. The same stillness I felt underwater that day. The same presence. The same strange calm. I didn't need to escape my life to find peace. I just needed to stop running from it.

Journal Prompt: What moment today did I almost miss because

I was worrying about the future? What beauty is right in front of me that I've been overlooking? What would it look like to truly believe that today is enough?

CHAPTER 5

TAKE EVERY THOUGHT CAPTIVE

"Attention passengers, please keep your seat belts fastened as we are just hitting turbulence," the intercom announces as I stare out the window on my way to a place I am completely unfamiliar with.

It is the summer right before my junior year of university begins, and the sales job I took to make some extra money, to help pay for my college education, so my parents would not have to stress all the time, is finally starting to get interesting.

Just a couple of months earlier, I had signed up for a sales training course to help sharpen my confidence because I had severe social anxiety. For some reason, I always had this thought in my mind that people found me annoying. That my friends were secretly embarrassed to be associated with me. That girls thought I was weird or talked about me behind my back and laughed because I looked different.

My anxiety was so bad that sometimes, when I went to the store to buy vegetables and the nice old lady handed me my change, I struggled to look her in the eyes. I was afraid she would somehow see the insecurities I wore on my sleeves. Sales felt like the complete opposite of who I was. And yet, for some reason, it ended up being one of the best things that ever happened to my anxious mind.

Of course, my mom and dad were disappointed. They wanted me to be a doctor, a dentist, a lawyer, or a nurse. Something they could brag about to their friends. Something that sounded respectable. Something that made sense in their world of status and security.

What good is telling your friends that your son is a salesman? That doesn't earn admiration. That doesn't impress anyone. And in their world, that mattered.

But for some reason, something in my heart felt right about it. I had always been afraid of talking to people. Eye contact. Public speaking. Speaking out of turn. Being in large groups. Having a bunch of people look at me. All of it terrified me. And yet, something inside me kept pulling me toward it.

Maybe it was because I didn't have the luxury of waiting for my dental career to take off. Maybe it was because my parents had recently gone through a house foreclosure that we tried to keep quiet out of pride. Or maybe it was something deeper. Maybe it was the part of me that was tired of hiding. The part that wanted to force that scared, anxious little boy out of his comfort zone so he could finally face real life instead of hiding in bed, oversleeping, and trying to escape the weight of responsibility as I grew older.

Sales became the gateway into understanding my own mind. Because with sales comes rejection. And with rejection comes self-judgment. And with self-judgment comes pain. And with pain, repeated enough times, comes suffering. And with enough suffering, paired with time and reflection, something begins to change.

Growth.

The more I pursued sales on the side, the more I started to outgrow the anxious version of myself. I was slowly becoming someone my parents and friends barely recognized. Not because I was pretending to be someone else, but because I was finally meeting parts of myself I had avoided my entire life.

For example, over the span of just a few months in my sales position, I went from shy, insecure, and afraid to look people in the eyes to becoming the top sales performer in my small town. I was always on the move, and my feet were moving too fast for my anxiety to catch up with me. I didn't have time to sit still long enough to remember how much I hated myself.

As my numbers increased, the higher-ups started paying attention. Since it was summer and I had more flexibility, they wanted to give me real-world experience. One of them called me one day and said, "Mike, have you ever been to Portugal?"

"No," I replied, silently thinking that I had never even left the country in my adult life, let alone traveled alone.

"Great," he said. "We're putting you on a plane in a couple of weeks. Pack your bags."

My jaw dropped.

Now, I'm sitting on the plane, wondering if I made a huge mistake. My parents were in disbelief that a company would fly me to Europe on their dime. My mom kept saying, "Be careful, they might try to kill you over there," half-joking, half-terrified.

She had always been afraid of me leaving the house. When I was younger, I was a sickly kid with allergies and random asthma attacks. She feared that if I went too far, something would happen and she wouldn't be there to save me.

And now, I'm sitting on this plane next to a sweet old lady who keeps offering me peanuts she doesn't want, and my mind starts spiraling. *What if I die out here? What if something happens and no one finds my body? What if I get kidnapped? What if I disappear and my parents never know what happened to me? If I died, how much would it break their hearts? Would I still feel guilty, even after I'm dead?*

Why am I worrying about the guilt I would feel *after* I die?

My thoughts race faster and faster as the turbulence starts to hit. I take a deep breath and try to quiet my mind.

Stillness.

And then I hear it.

That voice.

The devilish imp.

It's been a while since I've been still enough to notice him, so I guess he's been running wild in the background while I thought I had already done the work. I thought I was past this. Apparently not.

I realize this isn't a one-time battle. It's a constant practice, a daily awareness. A decision to observe instead of react. To look inward instead of being dragged around by my thoughts.

I look at him in the eye of my mind. He looks like me, but twisted. A distorted version of myself with a devilish grin.

And the strange thing is, the more I sit in stillness and shine the flashlight of awareness on him, the more distorted he becomes. His face warps. His voice shifts. Sometimes it's low. Sometimes high. Sometimes it jumps around like a cartoon character, trying to entertain and terrify me at the same time.

That's the dangerous part. When he sounds the most like me, that's when he has the most power. That's when I believe him.

But when I really look at him, when I observe instead of react, I start to see that he isn't me at all. The voice wobbles. The face distorts. And suddenly, I can tell the difference. And in that moment, he loses control.

It's exhausting work. Constant. But the more I practice it, the stronger that muscle in the eye of my mind becomes. The muscle that separates truth from fear. The part of me that can watch instead of panic. The part that can choose instead of reacting.

And slowly, I begin to realize that freedom doesn't come from silencing the voice forever. It comes from recognizing that it was never me to begin with. As I hold the neck of the devilish imp in my mind, watching it squirm and struggle to break free, I decide to ask it a question.

"Whose voice do you belong to?" I ask. "And why do you sound like me?"

The devilish imp freezes. It covers its mouth as if afraid it has already said too much. Then, slowly, a voice slips out, clear as day.

"Be careful, they may try to kill you when you land."

Mom?

Why does this voice sound like my mom now?

Before I can process it, the voice shifts again.

"Shut up, Mike. You don't understand. Just sit quietly while your mother and I figure out how to pay the bills this month."

Dad?

Why do you sound like my dad now?

I grip the devilish imp tighter as more voices spill out of it, one after another, each one painfully familiar. *Don't end up like your father. Money is the root of all evil. Suffering and destroying our health is how we show you we love you. Alcohol is the key to solving your problems. When you love someone, and you disagree, you yell louder. Whoever lasts the longest wins. Stop talking and sit down. You're so weak. You're sickly.*

My chest tightens.

The imp is screaming all the insecurities I've carried deep in my bones for as long as I can remember. But this time, something is different. This time, I'm watching it instead of being swallowed by it.

The voice doesn't sound like *me* anymore.

It sounds like my mom when I was five, snapping at me under the weight of exhaustion and stress. It sounds like my dad when he hit me with his belt for disobeying him. It sounds like the kids at school laughing at how I looked, how small I was, how different I seemed. It sounds like doctors calling me sickly and weak, as if my body itself was a problem to be fixed.

And suddenly, it hits me. These aren't my thoughts. These are echoes, fragments of other people's fear, pain, and unresolved trauma that lodged themselves inside me when I was too young to know the difference. This devilish imp wasn't born inside me. It was built. Piece by piece. Word by word. Scar by scar.

It fed on the things said to me when I was small and powerless, and it learned how to mimic my voice so I would believe it was me.

And that's when the realization landed. This thing didn't *own* me. It didn't *define* me. It was never my true voice at all.

It was a collector of pain, a parasite that survived by convincing me it was my own mind speaking. And the moment I saw it clearly, really saw it, its power weakened. Because lies lose their grip the moment they are named. Then, for the first time, I could tell the difference between the voice that tried to break me and the voice that had been quietly waiting underneath all along.

As I sat there, watching that inner voice unravel before me, something deeper began to settle in. I started to realize that the real battle was never about silencing thoughts. It was about learning which ones deserved my attention in the first place. I had spent so many years believing that every thought that showed up in my mind deserved a seat at the table. If it appeared, I assumed it must be true. If it felt loud, I believed it must be important. If it scared me, I assumed it must be warning me of something real.

But standing there, watching that distorted voice twist and flicker, I started to understand something new. Not every thought was mine. Not every voice deserved my obedience. That's when a line I had heard before finally landed differently in my chest. *"Be transformed by the renewing of your mind." – Romans 12:2.* Not by controlling everything. Not by suppressing emotion. But by renewing. By choosing what gets renewed and what gets released. I realized that my mind had been running on old programming for years, inherited fears, borrowed shame, and secondhand beliefs passed down from people who were just trying to survive themselves.

Some of those thoughts were just noise. Some were echoes. Some were fear dressed up as wisdom. Some were trauma wearing the mask of logic. And some were just lies that have been repeated so many times they start to sound like the truth.

The culture I grew up in taught me to dump everything out. To vent. To spiral. To express every emotion as if expression itself was healing. But Scripture was teaching me something quieter and much more grounded. It was teaching me to filter, to test, to pause.

"Do not believe every spirit, but test the spirits to see whether they are from God." – 1 John 4:1. That line hit me differently once I realized that thoughts are not neutral. Some build. Some decay. Some pull you toward the truth. Others pull you toward fear and paralysis. The work wasn't to silence my mind, but to become the gatekeeper of it.

I couldn't always stop a thought from knocking. But I could decide whether to open the door. That's when the story of David and Goliath started making sense to me in a way it never had before. I had always heard it as a story about bravery or strength. But now I saw it as a story about perception. Everyone else saw the same giant and panicked. The same armor. The same size. The same threat. *"When the Israelites saw the man, they all fled from him in great fear." – 1 Samuel 17:24.*

But David saw something different. He didn't deny the size of the giant. He just didn't let it define the outcome. He didn't focus on the problem. He focused on who stood beside him. The battlefield didn't change. The enemy didn't shrink. What changed was where

David placed his attention.

That's when it hit me. My anxiety wasn't proof that something was wrong with me. It was just evidence that I had been staring at the giant too long. Feeding it. Studying it. Letting it narrate the story. And the more I stared at it, the bigger it felt.

What I was learning was this: what you feed grows, and what you starve weakens. Every time I chose to dwell on fear, it grew muscles. Every time I rehearsed worst-case scenarios, they gained weight. But when I turned my attention toward truth, even briefly, something shifted. The fear didn't vanish instantly, but it lost authority.

That's when I realized I wasn't called to manage every thought. I was called to master my attention. To choose what gets airtime. To decide what story I live inside of. I didn't need to conquer my mind in one heroic moment. I just needed to notice when a thought didn't belong to me and let it pass by without bowing to it. And slowly, with practice, the battlefield started to change.

Not because the noise disappeared, but because I finally knew which voice was worth listening to. That realization didn't make everything peaceful overnight. It didn't suddenly make my mind quiet or my fears vanish. What it did give me was a way to respond. A way to stop being dragged around by every thought that showed up uninvited. I started to understand that freedom wasn't the absence of noise. It was discernment.

At first, I didn't even know how to do that. I had spent most of my life believing that every thought in my head was *me*. If it sounded like me, if it felt emotional, if it came with urgency or fear, I assumed it must be true. But slowly, almost awkwardly, I began practicing something new.

When a fearful or shame-filled thought appeared, I stopped treating it like a command and started treating it like a question. I would literally pause and say to myself, *What is this?* Where did this come from? And more importantly, *does this sound like something God would say to me?*

At first, it felt forced, unnatural, almost fake. But over time, I realized that this pause was power. This pause was the gap where choice lived. Instead of immediately spiraling, I learned to name the thought. Fear. Shame. Control. Catastrophe. Then I learned to challenge it. Not with optimism. Not with denial. But with truth.

I started replacing the lies with words that carried weight. Words that had survived centuries of human fear and suffering. Scriptures I had heard before but never actually used. Verses I began to memorize not as religious homework, but as lifelines. Tools. Weapons.

When my mind whispered, *You're going to fail,* something else would rise quietly inside me: *"The Lord is my shepherd; I shall not want."* When fear said, *You're not enough,* another voice answered, *"My grace is sufficient for you."* When anxiety told me everything was about to fall apart, I remembered, *"Do not be anxious about tomorrow, for tomorrow will worry about itself."* I wasn't trying to be holy. I was trying to survive. And somehow, these words met me exactly where I was.

Over time, I built little checkpoints throughout my day. Not rigid rituals. Just moments of honesty. I would stop and ask myself, *Is this thought helping me live, or is it pulling me deeper into fear?* If it was the latter, I didn't argue with it. I just didn't let it drive.

That's when I began to understand something I'd never been taught growing up. Not every thought deserves attention. Some thoughts are like strangers knocking on your door. You don't have to invite them in just because they showed up.

And then there was this question that changed everything for me. I started asking this question whenever a thought felt heavy, cruel, or condemning: *Would Jesus say this to me?* Not the version of Jesus I'd been afraid of as a kid. Not the angry one I imagined keeping score. But the one who sat with outcasts. The one who touched the untouchable. The one who spoke with firmness and gentleness at the same time.

And almost every time, the answer was no.

He wouldn't tell me I was weak. He wouldn't shame me for being afraid. He wouldn't rush me, threaten me, or humiliate me into change. So, if the voice in my head didn't sound like that, I learned to let it pass.

That's when I realized something profound. This wasn't about silencing my mind. It was about training my attention. About choosing what I feed. About learning that my inner world needed leadership, not suppression.

The more I practiced, the clearer it became. I didn't need to fight my thoughts. I needed to filter them. I needed to become a steward of my inner life. To guard the door. To decide which voices were allowed to stay and which ones had overstayed their welcome.

And slowly, almost quietly, something shifted. The noise didn't vanish, but it lost its authority. The fear still showed up, but it no longer ran the house. And for the first time, I felt something new forming inside me. Not control. Clarity. And in that clarity, I started to sense the presence of something steady beneath it all. A voice that didn't shout. A presence that didn't rush. A peace that didn't depend on everything going right. A voice that had been there the whole time, patiently waiting for me to stop listening to everything else.

Journal Prompt: What thoughts have been ruling my emotions lately? Write down the top 3. For each one, ask: Is this thought true? Is it helpful? Does it sound like the voice of God?

CHAPTER 6

LET IT GO LET IT DIE

"I slept with someone else." I stare at her bright blue eyes as she says it, sitting across from me in our favorite lunch spot, the one we used to go to every Sunday. A sharp pain hits my stomach, the kind that feels like someone reached down my throat and shoved my heart into my gut. My chest tightens, and breathing becomes more and more difficult.

I'm lying on a couch in the apartment of my friend Andre, a random sales rep I met while living in Portugal, trying to sleep so I can be rested for an important presentation I have to lead the next day. But all I can think about is the last conversation I had with my ex before I flew out of the country.

I toss and turn. I switch pillows. I adjust my body over and over again. I beg and bargain with my subconscious to please just turn off so I can sleep until morning. But nothing works. My mind refuses to quiet.

Instead, the devilish imp is there with me, hanging out in the darkness. My thoughts crawl across the ceiling like a movie being projected, one painful scene after another, looping endlessly while I lie there wide awake.

All I can think about is her. What did I do to deserve this? I thought we were going to get married. I thought we were going to have kids. I thought we were going to grow old together after traveling the world. Now, that future I had pictured so clearly is dead.

Maybe if I were rich, she would have stayed. Maybe if I hadn't studied so hard for my dental exams and had spent more time with her, she wouldn't have left. Maybe if I had asked her to move in with me, I could have watched who came into her life and protected her from other men. Should I have been more protective? Should I have spoken up sooner? Maybe she was ashamed of dating me. Maybe she realized how much of a people pleaser I am and lost attraction. Maybe I just suck as a human being.

My thoughts start racing faster and faster.

"SHUT UP!" I say out loud to the devilish imp.

The devilish imp laughs, pleased that he has the upper hand in my mind for this round of the battle. I start spiraling about how this will affect my performance tomorrow and how I'm going to fail at the event. How I'll disappoint everyone the same way I've disappointed everyone I've ever loved. The thoughts pile on top of each other until they feel unbearable.

I toss and turn for hours, unable to escape my own head, until I finally notice the dim light of the morning sun creeping through the corner of the window in the place I'm staying. The night has passed, and I'm still awake, still trapped inside the storm of my mind.

"It's the best we have," Andre says, as he shows me the event space. It's a musty old basketball gym that's been booked for the Saturday training.

I look around the room and feel a wave of disappointment wash over me. This wasn't what I imagined when I thought about traveling the world and speaking on stages. This wasn't the vision. The floor is scuffed, the lights are harsh, and the air feels stale. Nothing about it feels inspiring.

Slowly, people begin to file in. Sales reps from all over Portugal take their seats, curious to learn from the guy who flew in from America to teach them sales.

And that's when it hits me.

The imposter syndrome creeps in quietly at first, then louder with every person who walks through the door. The devilish imp wakes up and starts whispering in my ear.

"You're going to mess this up."

"They don't respect you."

"Why would they listen to you when the person you loved most in the world didn't even respect you enough to stay faithful?"

The words sink deep. Each new face feels like another judgment. Another reason I don't belong here. Another reminder that maybe I'm pretending to be someone I'm not.

I stand there, watching the room fill, feeling the weight of every doubt stack on my chest, knowing the imp is feeding on my fear, waiting for me to collapse under it.

Oh, how tired I am. I am so tired that I let the devilish imp sway me around for a moment as my anxiety and nervousness rise with every new face that walks into the gym.

I sit down in the corner and pull out my journal. If I can't catch the thoughts with my mind, maybe I can trap them on the page. Maybe if I write them down, I can pin the devilish imp there long enough to breathe. Maybe if I give the chaos somewhere to go, it will stop bouncing around inside me.

Andre has already gathered everyone and started the first half of the training session. I can hear his voice echoing through the gym, confident and steady.

The devilish imp goes on the attack, sensing weakness, sensing fear, knowing my turn is coming. "You are a fraud. You are an imposter. You are not confident. You are a loser."

My hands shake slightly as I write faster, trying to keep up with the thoughts before they consume me. I need to get them out of my head and onto the page, somewhere I can see them instead of feel them.

Then Andre speaks again.

"I want to introduce you to a successful, well-respected person in the sales space who came all the way from America to teach us today." The devilish imp laughs louder now, almost gleeful, feeding on my panic. I scribble furiously, writing every word it throws at me, trying to drain it out of my mind before I have to stand up and face the room.

"Give a round of applause for Mike Vestil," Andre says loudly, as I snap my journal shut, trapping the devilish imp inside its pages at the very last second.

I stand up.

I look around.

I see all these unfamiliar faces staring back at me with curious, eager eyes. I feel the anxiety rise in my chest, that familiar tightness crawling upward toward my throat. My heart starts racing. My palms get warm. The old fear shows up right on time.

I pause.

I take one deep breath in.

Then I let it all out in one slow exhale, releasing as much of the worry as I can. And then my mouth starts moving, repeating the words my mentor once taught me, almost on autopilot.

"Okay, guys, look around the gym. How many things do you see that are brown? Look for brown. Look for brown. Look for brown. Count them. How many do you see?"

The twenty people in the room begin scanning the space, their eyes darting around as they silently count all the brown things they can find.

"Close your eyes," I say.

They listen.

"Now, tell me, how many things did you see that were blue?"

Silence.

"Who here can confidently tell me?" I ask.

Still silence.

"Okay, open your eyes. Now, how many blue things do you see?"

Almost instantly, people start calling them out. Someone points to my blue dress shirt. Others begin naming blue objects around the room. Within seconds, they're listing them off with certainty.

I chuckle a little.

It's only been a couple of months since someone did this exercise on me, and now I'm watching their eyes widen the same way mine did. Like I just pulled off some kind of magic trick.

"You see," I say, "in life, we have this thing called the reticular activation system. It's the part of our brain that scans our environment for what we believe is important."

I pause and look around the room.

"The problem is that part of our mind gets programmed. And a lot of us were programmed by people who were anxious, fearful, or constantly focused on what was wrong. So, we grow up trained to look for the brown. The problems. The threats. The things that confirm our fears."

I gesture around the room again.

"And when something blue shows up, when opportunity or beauty or possibility is right in front of us, we don't even see it. Not because it isn't there, but because our mind is too busy scanning for danger."

I feel my chest loosen as I speak. The imp is quiet now. It's watching, listening.

"And that's how most people live their lives," I continue. "Not because the world is bad, but because they've been trained to look for the worst parts of it."

As I spoke those words out loud, I realized how healing it was for me to teach them. In that moment, teaching was doing more for me than it was for anyone sitting in that room. I could feel the shift happening inside me as I spoke. I could feel the devilish imp stirring, trying to bring up everything it usually used against me. The girl I loved leaving me for someone else. The infidelity. The shame. The guilt I carried for disappointing my parents. My constant need to be perfect. The endless replaying of my past mistakes.

And suddenly, I saw it clearly.

All of that was just the color brown.

Those were the things my mind had been trained to look for. The failures. The losses. The moments that hurt. The stories that kept me small. And because I kept focusing on them, I couldn't see the blue that was right in front of me. The growth. The opportunity. The healing. The life that was happening now.

I realized in that moment that the past cannot be fixed, changed, or rewritten. It can only be released. And if I wanted my future to live, then my attachment to the old version of myself had to die. The shame. The regret. The identity built around pain. All of it had to be laid down so something new could be born.

"You see," I continued, "the reason the reticular activation system is so important is that your mind works like a thermostat. When it gets too hot, the AC turns on. When it gets too cold, the heater kicks in. It always returns to its set point."

Everyone nodded.

"The problem is that the set point wasn't chosen by us. It was given to us. Programmed into us by the people who raised us."

I paused and looked around the room.

"One of the biggest ones is money. How many of you have noticed that no matter how much you make, your bank account always seems to return to the same number?"

Almost everyone nodded, some laughing in disbelief.

"That's not random," I said. "That's your financial thermostat. And if you don't change who controls that thermostat, it will keep pulling you back to the same level over and over again."

I let the words settle before continuing.

"And it's not just money. It's how we talk to ourselves. How we handle failure. How we respond to fear. How we define success. All of it is inherited. From our parents. From their fears. From their survival patterns. From the environments we grew up in."

I could feel the devilish imp stirring inside me, growing irritated.

"Shut up," it hissed. "You're exposing too much. They're going to wake up."

I looked at it with my mind's eye. For the first time, it looked small. Cornered.

"Who set your thermostat?" I asked the room. "Your mom? Your dad? Their stress? Their fears? Their coping mechanisms? Their unhealed wounds?"

Silence.

"And here's the truth," I continued. "Until you become aware of who set it, it will keep running your life."

I could feel the imp shrinking as I spoke. It hated this. It hated being seen.

"The moment you become aware of it," I said, "you get a choice. You can keep living on autopilot, or you can choose to reset it."

The room was still. Heavy. Present.

I felt something shift inside me too.

As I spoke, as I taught, as I told the truth out loud, I felt the devilish imp lose its grip. It no longer had a seat at the table. It no longer controlled the narrative. The more I spoke, the quieter it became.

And I could see it in their faces too. Recognition. Relief. Understanding. Because when we let the old thoughts die, something else gets to be born.

And in that moment, standing there in that gym, I realized something simple and profound: healing doesn't come from fighting the darkness. It comes from turning on the light.

As I absorbed all of this, something else began to surface. A quieter realization. One that didn't come with fireworks or certainty, but with a strange sense of release. I started to see that perhaps I had been trying to *resurrect* things that were never meant to live again.

I had spent so much of my life trying to fix the past. Replaying it. Rewriting it. Imagining alternate endings where I said the right thing, chose the right path, and became the right version of myself sooner. I thought healing meant understanding everything that happened to me. I thought peace came from solving the puzzle of my pain.

But the more I sat with myself, the more I realized something uncomfortable. Some things don't need to be solved. Some things need to be buried.

I came across a verse that hit me harder than I expected. *"Unless a seed falls into the ground and dies, it remains alone. But if it dies, it produces much fruit." – John 12:24.*

At first, I didn't like that. It felt too final. Too irreversible. I didn't want parts of me to die. I wanted them redeemed, fixed, and validated. I wanted to carry them forward like proof that my suffering meant something. But the truth started to settle in slowly. Maybe healing isn't about dragging every old version of myself into the future. Maybe it's about letting certain versions finally rest.

I realized I had been dragging entire versions of myself forward like ghosts. The boy who wanted approval. The teenager who felt unseen. The man who believed love had to be earned through achievement. I kept trying to bring them with me, to explain them, justify them, protect them. But they were heavy. And they were tired.

Another line kept echoing in my mind. *"Forget the former things; do not dwell on the past." – Isaiah 43:18–19.* That word forget doesn't mean erase. It means stop living there. Stop setting up camp in a place you were only meant to pass through.

I started to understand that God was not asking me to dissect my pain forever. He wasn't asking me to analyze it until I bled inside. He was asking me to trust Him enough to let some things go unfinished. Unanswered. Unredeemed in the way I wanted. Because resurrection doesn't come from obsession. It comes from surrender.

I kept thinking about the image of a burial. How strange it is that something so full of life has to be placed underground first. Hidden. Covered. Left alone. We think death is the end, but in nature, death is often a beginning in disguise.

Jesus didn't rise immediately. There were days of silence. No miracles. No explanations. Just stillness. From the outside, it looked like loss. Like failure. Like the story had ended the wrong way. But something sacred was happening beneath the surface. And that's when it hit me. Maybe my own life had those quiet days too. Those in-between moments where nothing seemed to be happening. Where I felt stuck, behind, forgotten. Maybe those weren't delays. Maybe they were burials.

I had been trying to dig up things God was asking me to lay down. Old dreams. Old versions of success. Old identities built around fear and proving myself. I wanted them to come back to life on my terms. But growth doesn't work that way. *"There is a time to mourn. A time to uproot. A time to let go." – Ecclesiastes 3:1-6.* That line stopped feeling poetic and started feeling painfully practical. Some dreams have to die so better ones can grow. Some seasons have to end so new ones can begin. Some versions of me had to be buried so the next version could breathe. And maybe that's why peace only came when I stopped trying to control the resurrection. Because resurrection isn't something you manufacture; it's something you allow.

I started to see that faith wasn't about clinging harder. It was about trusting the process of decay and renewal, about believing that what looks like an ending might actually be preparation.

If God didn't rush the resurrection, why was I rushing mine? So, I began to let things go. Slowly. Gently. Without drama. I stopped trying to carry every memory, every mistake, every dream that no longer fit. I let them rest. And in the quiet that followed, something new began to breathe. Not loud. Not flashy. Just alive.

And for the first time, that felt like enough.

That's when I started realizing something else. Healing wasn't going to come from thinking harder or understanding more. It was going to come from practicing release. From doing small, intentional things that taught my nervous system it was safe to let go.

I didn't wake up one day suddenly free. I had to learn how to forgive in motion. I started with something simple. I would sit alone, sometimes with a candle lit, sometimes just with a pen and paper, and I would talk to the version of myself I had spent years resenting. The one who didn't know better. The one who made choices out of fear. The one who tried to survive with the tools he had. I would say it out loud, even when it felt awkward. "I forgive you. I release you. I don't need you to be perfect to move forward." Sometimes I cried. Sometimes I felt nothing. But something inside me softened every time I said it.

Then I started doing something that felt strange at first but slowly became sacred. I would write down the things I couldn't stop carrying. Regrets. Old shame. Moments I replayed in my head like evidence against myself. And instead of analyzing them, I let them go physically. I tore the paper. I burned it. Sometimes I buried it in the ground. I needed my body to understand what my mind couldn't yet accept. That some things were not meant to be carried forever. Some things were meant to return to the earth.

I also realized that peace doesn't just happen by accident. It has to be practiced. I started treating stillness like a discipline. I made space in my day where I wasn't allowed to fix the past or plan the future. No replaying conversations. No rewriting old scenes. Just being. Sitting. Breathing. Letting the present moment be enough. At first, it felt uncomfortable, almost irresponsible. But slowly, my nervous system began to trust that nothing bad would happen if I stopped trying to control everything.

And then there was prayer. Not the kind I grew up with, where I asked God to fix things or make my life easier. This was different. Quieter. More honest. Sometimes all I could say was, "God, take what I lost and make something beautiful from it, even if I never get to see how." That sentence became an offering. A release of ownership. A surrender of outcomes.

I stopped asking for answers and started asking for alignment. I stopped demanding explanations and started asking for trust. I realized that maybe faith wasn't about understanding the story, but about trusting the Author.

And slowly, almost imperceptibly, something shifted. I wasn't trying to resurrect the past anymore. I wasn't dragging old versions of myself forward. I was learning to walk lighter. To let grief be grief. To let growth take time. To believe that even what was buried was still part of something sacred.

That's when I understood that healing isn't loud. It doesn't announce itself. It doesn't rush in with fireworks. Sometimes it just shows up quietly and says, "You can rest now."

Journal Prompt: What is one regret or "what if" that you keep replaying in your mind? What have you been trying to fix that maybe God is asking you to bury?

CHAPTER 7

YOU DON'T NEED TO KNOW EVERYTHING

"Don't end up like your father." That thought keeps looping in my mind through the mouth of the devilish imp.

Why does it stay there? What is it about my father that I'm so afraid of becoming? I love my dad. I really do. So why does my mom seem so afraid that I might turn out like him? Is it because she thinks he failed? Because she never felt safe enough to relax, always worried he might go on another drinking spree? Is it because she doesn't trust that he could provide for the family the way she needed him to?

Where does all of this come from? And why does my mind spiral every time the devilish imp brings it up? I've grown used to him now. My unwanted roommate. The voice that never leaves. The one that lives in my head and never shuts up.

The next morning, I wake up early to a phone call from my mom.

"Baby."

"Yes, Mom. Is everything okay?"

I can hear it in the silence before she answers. Something is wrong. The pause stretches on longer than it should.

"Can you please come home this weekend? We need help moving our belongings."

"Why, Mom? Is everything okay? What's happening?"

Another pause. Then her voice breaks.

"We can't afford the mortgage anymore. It's too hard with all the bills, especially with your schooling. We want you to be a dentist, so we have to downsize now."

Foreclosure.

My childhood home. The walls that held my memories. The place I thought would always be there. Gone. Just like that.

I slam the door shut on my beat-up brown Honda Civic and pull onto the highway for the two-hour drive back home. When I arrive, I see my mom sitting there with her face buried in her hands, as if someone has died. I wonder how long she's been like this. Since this morning? Since we talked on the phone? She looks exhausted. Hollowed out.

"Mom, do you want some water?" I ask.

"No, my dear. I'm fine."

But I can feel it in my gut. Something is wrong. A deep uneasiness settles in my stomach. Guilt. Heavy and familiar.

That night, I sleep on the bottom bunk in my old room, the same bed I slept in as a kid. I stare up at the ceiling, wondering if these are the last moments I'll ever have in this house. The walls feel different now. Like they already know they're about to be emptied. As I lie there, the familiar spirals return, projecting my fears and insecurities across the ceiling like a movie I've seen too many times.

Then the devilish imp appears again, grinning.

"It's your fault your mom is like this," he says. "You're such a burden. If you were dead, she wouldn't be this stressed."

"Shut up," I whisper, not wanting to deal with him tonight.

I turn onto my side, hoping sleep will take me. It doesn't. My thoughts race. What do I do now? If I become a dentist, the stress might kill my mom anyway. If I drop out and chase something uncertain, all the sacrifices my parents made will have been for nothing. All the nights they worked. All the exhaustion. All the fear. I imagine the heartbreak on her face if I told her I was walking away.

Either way, it feels like someone loses. What do I do? I honestly have no idea.

It seemed like up until this point, I really didn't have to think. Becoming a dentist felt like my destiny ever since I was thirteen. Because of that, I didn't have to make real choices. I could just kick the can of suffering down the road and tell myself I would deal with the consequences later. I thought I had time.

But it turns out that the tax came due much earlier than I expected. Either way, someone was going to suffer.

Guilt. Guilt. Guilt. *What do I do? What do I do? What do I do?*

The devilish imp starts circling the ceiling of my mind, laughing as he watches me spiral. What happens if I continue dentistry? My parents become even more stressed. I become more stressed. I spend my twenties buried in a library or trapped in a dental office. I drown in debt I can barely comprehend. I tell myself it will magically disappear by the time I'm in my forties.

Maybe I survive long enough to see that day. Or maybe the stress kills me first. Or maybe I live, but my marriage doesn't. Maybe my wife grows resentful of my absence. Maybe she feels like she settled. Maybe I keep people-pleasing until there's nothing left of me. Maybe she loses attraction. Maybe she takes her anger out on me. And maybe, because I feel so powerless, I take that anger out on my future kids.

And then it hits me. This feels familiar. This feels like déjà vu. This feels like my childhood. This feels like my dad. If I go down this path, I don't just become a dentist. I become him.

So, do I disrespect my mom and do the complete opposite? To not listen to her? But then I'll be a bad son. That also isn't good.

I try to control the situation with my thoughts, but it goes nowhere. The devilish imp laughs hysterically as my face tightens from thinking so hard. Think. Think. Think. Thoughts. Thoughts. Thoughts. And suddenly the sun is coming up.

What the heck? Have I really been thinking for the past eight hours? I'm so tired. What do I do? If I leave dental school, then what? Do I just remain a salesman? But what if there is no stability? What if I can't make a sale? What if I end up a failure?

"Don't end up like your father." My mom's voice echoes in my mind.

"Stability. Safe. It's what people do."

The words repeat over and over in her voice, looping inside my head. But the fear of leaving something that has been so deeply tied to my identity grips me. What if I'm not good enough? What if I mess up? What if I disappoint my future wife and kids because I couldn't provide as my dad did?

And then, out of nowhere, a different voice enters. It isn't mine. It isn't the devilish imp. All it says, in a calm, steady tone, is one word.

"Trust."

I blink. It's 1 p.m. I had slept the deepest sleep I have ever slept after that voice spoke. It was as if something inside my heart finally let go of needing a plan, or control, or certainty about the future. I touched my chest and remembered how I felt when I heard that voice.

Peace. Calm. Is this what that feels like?

That Monday, I drove back to the university. I walked into the office, looked at the counselor, and said I was withdrawing my seat from dental school. I didn't understand it at first, but that moment changed something in me. Not because everything suddenly made sense, but because I finally stopped demanding that it had to. Up until then, I thought faith meant having answers. I thought it meant clarity. A plan. A timeline. Something I could point to and say, "See, this is why I'm doing this." I thought God would hand me a map if I just tried hard enough or proved myself worthy enough.

But that isn't what happened.

What happened was silence. Not the scary kind. It was the steady kind. The kind that doesn't explain, but somehow steadies you anyway.

That's when I started to understand what the verse meant when it says, *"The secret things belong to the Lord." – Deuteronomy 29:29.* I used to read that and feel frustrated. Like God was withholding something from me. Like He was hiding the answers just out of reach. But now, I hear it differently. Maybe it wasn't about secrets I wasn't allowed to know. Maybe it was about freedom. About not needing to carry the weight of knowing everything.

I had spent so long trying to think my way into safety. Trying to outsmart uncertainty. Trying to predict pain before it could touch me. But the truth was no amount of thinking ever made me feel safe. It only made me tired.

That's when another verse started to make sense in a way it never had before. *"We walk by faith, not by sight." – 2 Corinthians 5:7.*

I used to think that meant blind belief. Blind obedience. Blind religion. But standing there, having just walked away from the most carefully planned future of my life, I realized it meant something else entirely.

It meant that sometimes you move without knowing where the ground will land beneath your foot. Not because you're reckless, but because staying still would slowly kill you. Faith, I was learning, is not about certainty. It's about trust. Not trust that everything will work out the way you want, but trust that you will be held even if it doesn't.

I kept thinking about how obsessed I had been with understanding everything before taking a step. I wanted guarantees. Proof. Insurance against regret. But life doesn't offer that. And neither does God.

"Trust in the Lord with all your heart and lean not on your own understanding." – Proverbs 3:5. That line used to irritate me. It felt like an excuse not to think. But now, I hear it differently. It isn't telling me to abandon my mind. It's telling me not to worship it.

My mind had become my god. My safety. My compass. And it had led me straight into exhaustion. I realized I had been treating life like a math equation. If I could just get enough variables right, I could control the outcome. But life isn't math. It's more like walking in the dark with just enough light for the next step.

And that's when the story of Abraham finally clicked for me. God didn't give him a map. He didn't give him coordinates, a timeline, or a backup plan. He just said, "Go." And Abraham went. Not because he knew where he was going, but because he trusted who was calling him. That hit me hard. I had been waiting for certainty before moving, but faith was asking me to move before certainty arrived. Not recklessly. Not blindly. But humbly.

I began to see that maybe the reason God didn't give me a full plan was that a full plan would have kept me in control. And control had become my addiction. Clarity feeds ego. Dependence feeds faith.

I didn't need to know how it would all work out. I just needed to take the next honest step. The one that felt aligned rather than forced. The one that didn't require me to betray myself to feel safe.

For the first time, I stopped asking, "What's the smartest move?"

And I started asking, "What's the truest one?"

And the answer didn't come as a strategy, a spreadsheet, or a five-year plan. It came as a quiet sense of direction. A gentle nudge. A deep yes in my chest that didn't need to explain itself. I didn't know where I was going. But I knew I was finally walking. And somehow, that was enough.

Modern Mindset vs. Biblical Wisdom

Modern Mindset	Biblical Wisdom
"If it's unclear, don't act yet."	"Abraham obeyed… not knowing where." (Hebrews 11:8)
"Get all the answers first."	"The secret things belong to the Lord." (Deut. 29:29)
"Clarity brings peace."	"The peace of God surpasses understanding." (Philippians 4:7)
"You have to control the outcome."	"God establishes your steps." (Proverbs 16:9)
"Uncertainty is dangerous."	"Uncertainty is where dependence grows."
"Knowledge is power."	"The fear of the Lord is the beginning of wisdom." (Proverbs 9:10)

That realization didn't magically make the fear disappear. It didn't suddenly make life simple or clear. What it did was change how I related to the fear. Instead of trying to outrun it or solve it, I started learning how to walk with it without letting it lead me.

I began to notice something about myself. When I tried to wait for total certainty, I froze. I would overthink until I was exhausted, then punish myself for being tired. I kept telling myself I needed more clarity before I could move, but the truth was I was hiding behind that need. Clarity had become my excuse to distrust.

So, I started practicing something new. Something uncomfortable. I stopped waiting for perfect certainty and started listening for enough peace. Not confidence. Not excitement. Just enough peace to take one honest step. I told myself, "You don't need to know everything. You just need to know the next right thing." That alone felt rebellious. Like I was breaking some internal rule I had lived by my whole life.

I started setting limits on my decisions. Not deadlines, but boundaries. I would give myself a window to pray, think, journal, and sit with something. Then I would choose. Not because I felt one hundred percent sure, but because I felt at least seventy percent calm. The rest I would hand over to God.

It felt reckless at first. Like walking without checking the ground. But something surprising happened. The moment I stopped demanding certainty, my body softened. My chest loosened. My thoughts slowed down. I wasn't calm because I had answers. I was calm because I stopped trying to be my own savior.

I also began writing things down. Not to solve them, but to release them. I would take out my journal and pour everything onto the page. Every fear. Every what if. Every possible disaster my mind could invent. And then, when I had nothing left to write, I would draw a line across the page and write one sentence beneath it.

"These belong to God now."

Sometimes my hand would shake when I wrote it. Sometimes I

didn't believe it. But something about physically placing those thoughts outside of myself helped me breathe again. It was like setting down a heavy backpack I had been carrying for years and realizing I didn't have to pick it back up.

I also stopped asking God for full explanations. I started asking simpler questions.

"What is the next right step?"

Not the next five years. Not the backup plan. Just the next step that didn't betray my conscience or my peace.

Some days, that meant making a phone call I was scared to make. Some days, it meant resting when my old patterns told me to push. Some days, it meant doing nothing at all and trusting that stillness was not laziness but obedience.

I began to understand what people meant when they said faith is a walk, not a leap. It's a series of small acts of obedience that don't look impressive from the outside but slowly rewire you on the inside.

Every morning, before my thoughts could start racing, I started whispering a simple prayer out loud. "I don't need to know everything. I just need to know You."

Sometimes, that was all I could manage. No eloquence. No theology. Just surrender. And strangely, the more I practiced this, the quieter the chaos became. Not gone, but quieter. The devilish imp still showed up sometimes, but he no longer ran the house. He had lost his authority. He could talk, but he couldn't drive.

I began to see that faith wasn't about forcing myself to feel brave. It was about choosing to trust even while feeling afraid. It wasn't about eliminating uncertainty. It was about refusing to let uncertainty make my decisions for me.

And slowly, without realizing, I stopped asking, "What if this goes wrong?"

I started asking, "What if this is how I learn to trust?"

That question didn't give me answers. It gave me permission. Permission to move. Permission to grow. Permission to be human. And somehow, that was enough.

Journal Prompt: What are the top 3 questions or unknowns consuming your thoughts lately? What emotions are hiding behind your need for clarity? Fear, regret, control, grief?

CHAPTER 8

GET OUT OF YOUR HEAD

"Mom, I'm going to live in Las Vegas for 30 days."

"What? What do you mean?" She sounds confused. Only a couple of weeks ago, I had told her I was dropping out of dental school. She thought I was joking. I wasn't. The second thing she said back then was, "You'd better go back, or I'll have a heart attack and die, and it will all be your fault."

What does a son even say to his mom when she says something like that? The guilt starts gnawing at my insides. But the decision is already made. I already acted. I didn't think it through. I just moved. And now, there is no going back. It reminds me of when I walked onto that stage in the musty gym in Portugal. My mind was racing. My chest was tight. My thoughts were spiraling in every direction. But the moment I stood up and moved forward, something shifted. My mind slowed down.

Just the weekend before, I was out with a friend who was trying to introduce me to some girls he knew. He knew I was heartbroken because my girlfriend had cheated on me, and he genuinely felt bad for me. So, he pulled me out of my room, where all I had been doing was reading books, journaling, and trying to build some kind of morning and evening routine while I figured out what to do with my life. He knew I had been isolating, so he decided to get me out of the house.

As he introduced me to the girls, my heart started fluttering. Immediately, I panicked. They looked at me and smiled. The devilish imp showed up right on cue and whispered, "They think you're ugly. You should try doing something. Be louder. Pretend you're more confident than you are."

"Um, what is your name?" one of the girls asked.

I didn't even realize I had been standing there frozen, listening to the devilish imp give me instructions.

"Mike!" I blurted out, way too loud, like volume could somehow cover my insecurity.

She caught it immediately. The awkwardness. The desperation. The lack of grounding. I could see it in her eyes. She thought I was weird.

After about two minutes, I had nothing left to say. I just stood there, staring at the floor, while the girls whispered to each other.

"We have to go," they said apologetically and left.

I knew it was because I was trapped in my head. The whole night went like that. We moved from group to group. Rejection after rejection. Each one stacking on top of the last. My heart curled inward, shrinking, trying to protect itself from the constant sting of judgment. Rejection by women hurt more than rejection in sales. This one went straight to my core.

So, I drank.

I drank faster than I could think. It worked, at least for a while. The thoughts quieted. The devilish imp got drunk, too, slurring his words until he couldn't speak at all. I looked around. The room spun. I was losing control, but at least my mind was finally quiet.

I tried talking to more people. Nothing landed. Hours passed. I grew tired. Eventually, I walked out alone.

Outside, I looked up at the night sky. The moon was huge. Full. Bright. I leaned against the wall to steady myself. I was sobering up. It had been a couple of hours since my last drink, and with the sobriety came the flood.

Shame. Guilt. Fear. Worry. What? My negative spirals now? Here? Of all places?

I started crying. I hid in the corner, hoping no one would see me. I thought about how much easier life would be if my girlfriend hadn't cheated on me. Or if dental school were free. Or if I had been born rich. I cried and cried as the thoughts stacked on top of each other, my mind turning into a loud, chaotic party. The devilish imp was having the time of his life, running wild, laughing as I unraveled.

I pull out my phone. I type in "confidence and dating coach."

I recall glancing at a sales page. All I remember is thirty days. A rather large man with a big beard, telling me I could change my life if I just committed to thirty days of immersion and mastery. That if I gave myself fully to the process, I could become a new man. Thirty days. That's it. Thirty days it is.

I swipe my credit card. I book the flight. And before I can fully process what I've done, I'm getting into the car as my friend walks out to drive my sorry self home.

I wake up the next morning. Did I really just do that? Apparently, I did.

Without even thinking, I committed to leaving. I committed to something unknown, and now I'm standing in front of my mom, telling her that I'm going to Las Vegas for some "sales training bootcamp." Which, technically, it is. I'm standing there in disbelief that I actually made this decision without overthinking it to death. I didn't make a pros and cons list. I didn't read reviews. I didn't ask my parents what they thought. I didn't ask my friends for permission. I just did it.

Several weeks later, I land in Vegas for the first time. I'm barely twenty-one years old. Somehow, that makes it feel even more surreal. Vegas, of all places. It feels like a strange contradiction, coming here at this age. The nightlife is louder, brighter, and more chaotic than the small-town dive bars I was used to.

Nervousness starts creeping in. A couple of months ago, I was set on becoming a dentist. Now, here I am in Vegas. What am I even doing with my life?

I get a message from the coach telling me to meet him at a burrito restaurant down the street. It takes me about thirty minutes to walk there. As I walk, I take in the bright lights, the loud street vendors trying to sell me something, and the constant movement of people everywhere. What is this feeling? Is it fear? Is it nervousness? Is it excitement? It feels like all of it at once.

I walk into the restaurant and immediately see him. A large man with a red beard. He's wearing a long-sleeve shirt with the buttons undone far too low, chest hair spilling out, and his hair sticking out in every direction. In front of him are two massive burritos on a plate that looks way too small for them. The table itself looks like it might collapse under the weight of his presence.

I sit down across from him.

"You're Mike?" he asks with a grin.

"Yes," I say quietly, already staring at the plate instead of his eyes. Nervous. Unsure of what comes next. He looks at me for a moment, then smiles wider.

"Let's go."

He grabs both burritos with both hands as we immediately get up and leave the restaurant to go to the mall. I still awkwardly have my backpack on, all my things stuffed inside it. He doesn't care. He just points and says, "See that couple over there, the guy and the girl?"

"Yes," I respond.

"Go up there and say hi."

"But—"

Before I can finish my excuse, he pushes me forward.

I stumble toward them like an idiot, eyes wide, frozen like a deer caught in headlights. I stop right in front of them, completely blank. My heart is pounding. My mouth is dry. The couple looks at me, confused.

"Are you okay?" they ask.

"Um… yeah, I'm fine," I say. "Uh… my name is Mike. What's your name?" I reach my hand out awkwardly.

They look at each other, then back at me, and without saying much, they walk away.

Rejection.

It stings. It sinks deep. It's like something inside me whispers that I am not worthy. That I am less than the dirt on the ground. Less than the piece of gum stuck to the sidewalk that someone scrapes off their shoe without thinking. That was me every time I was rejected.

That, I guess, was my first day of boot camp. The man would point at a group of people and tell me to say hi. Then he would say to me to have my feet moving faster than my mind could think. That was the only mission for the day.

The first couple of moments were awkward. But I started realizing something. Between the action I told myself to take and the actual moment of my body moving, there was this space in my mind. A space where the devilish imp either grabbed hold of the story or didn't.

The longer I waited between thought and action, the easier it was for the devilish imp to take over and start spinning lies. "What if they punch me?" "What if she has a boyfriend?" "What if he beats me up?" "What if they laugh at me?" "What if they throw ice cubes at me?"

These thoughts were little doses of the same negative spirals I would experience at night. The same ones that kept me trapped in my head. But the more I trained my feet to move faster than my mind, the easier it became to overcome those thoughts and to create a space of stillness in my mind through motion.

That's when I learned that in order to get out of my head, I either needed to be completely still and observe it, which is what I had done before. But this was the first time that action and movement were what created stillness in my mind as well.

I look back now and see how I came to that realization. Every time I acted without thinking and threw myself into the unknown, I didn't give the devilish imp the space to start spinning his gears of overthinking. It never even had the chance to take control.

Action, paired with faith, became a way to quiet the chaos. It became a way to silence the noise before it could grow teeth. Action plus faith was an effective way to still the monkey mind that once controlled me.

And that's when something finally clicked for me. I started to see that my problem was not fear; it was hesitation disguised as wisdom. I kept telling myself I was being careful, thoughtful, and responsible. But deep down, I was just afraid to move unless I could guarantee the outcome. I wanted certainty before action. I wanted proof before faith.

And that is when I realized something that quietly unsettled me. Faith was never meant to wait for clarity. I used to think faith meant believing the right things, saying the right prayers, and having the right understanding. But what I began to see was that faith is not about knowing. It is about moving. It is about stepping forward while your hands are still shaking.

There is a verse that kept echoing in my mind during this season.

"Faith without works is dead." – James 2:17. I had read it before, but this time it landed differently. I always thought it meant that good behavior proved faith. But what I started to understand was this: faith that never moves is not faith at all. It is fear wearing religious clothing.

I had spent so long waiting to feel ready. Waiting to feel confident. Waiting to feel certain. Waiting for the fear to go away. And the truth was, the fear was never going to leave first. The movement had to come before the confidence.

Another line kept surfacing in my mind, one I had heard growing up but never really understood. *"Go in the strength you have." – Judges 6:14.* Not the strength you wish you had. Not the strength you think you should have. The strength you have right now.

That hit me hard. God was not asking me to be fearless. He was asking me to be willing. To move with trembling hands. To act while unsure. To step forward even when my legs felt weak.

I realized how often I had been disguising fear as wisdom. I told myself I was waiting for the right moment, the right clarity, the right sign. But in reality, I was just protecting myself from discomfort. I was waiting for a guarantee that does not exist.

Then I saw it clearly. God was not waiting for me to figure everything out. He was waiting for me to move. Another verse kept echoing through my mind like a quiet drumbeat. *"Whatever your hand finds to do, do it with all your might." – Ecclesiastes 9:10.* It did not say wait until you understand everything. It did not say wait until the fear is gone. It did not say wait until you are healed, confident, or certain. It said do it. Move. Act.

And suddenly, I saw how much of my life had been delayed not by lack of opportunity, but by overthinking disguised as responsibility. I thought I was being careful. I thought I was being mature. But in reality, I was hiding.

I began to see that obedience is often quiet and unglamorous. It looks like showing up when you feel unqualified. It looks like taking a step without a map. It looks like trusting that clarity comes after motion, not before it.

There is a story Jesus tells about a servant who was given a bag of silver. He was afraid to lose it, afraid to mess it up, so he buried it in the ground. When the master returned, the servant proudly gave it back untouched. And the master was not impressed. *"I was afraid, so I went and hid your talent in the ground." – Matthew 25:25.*

That line haunted me. Not because the servant failed, but because he never even tried. He chose safety over stewardship. He chose preservation over obedience. I saw myself in that servant. I had buried parts of myself out of fear, buried my courage, my voice, my calling. All in the name of being responsible. And suddenly, I understood something painful but freeing. God was not asking me to be perfect. He was asking me to move. Overthinking was not wisdom. It was a cage. Faith was not about having all the answers. It was about taking the next step even while trembling.

So, I stopped waiting to feel ready. I stopped trying to solve my entire life in my head. I stopped demanding guarantees from God before moving my feet. I started choosing motion over mastery. Obedience over overanalysis. Action over paralysis. Not reckless action. Not blind chaos. But humble movement in the direction my heart already knew was right. I did not need the full map. I only needed the next step. And once I took it, I realized something beautiful. God was already there.

Modern Mindset vs. Biblical Wisdom

Modern Mindset	Biblical Wisdom
"Wait until you're 100% ready."	"Go in the strength you have." (Judges 6:14)
"Clarity before motion."	"Faith without works is dead." (James 2:17)
"Don't act until it's perfect."	"Do not despise small beginnings." (Zechariah 4:10)
"Sit and visualize more."	"Whatever you do, work at it with all your heart." (Colossians 3:23)
"Preparation is everything."	"Obedience is better than sacrifice." (1 Samuel 15:22)
"Faith = mindset."	"Faith = movement."
"Safe is wise."	"Safe can be disobedient."

He was not waiting at the finish line. He was not watching from a distance. He was in the step itself. In the trembling yes. In the messy movement forward. I had spent so much of my life thinking faith meant clarity, but what I started to learn was that faith actually looks like motion before understanding. It looks like obedience without a full explanation. It looks like choosing to move while still scared.

I began to notice a pattern in my own life. Every time I waited until I felt ready, nothing happened. I stayed stuck. I stayed trapped in my head, negotiating with fear, trying to reason my way into courage. But every time I moved first, something shifted. The fear didn't disappear, but it lost its grip. The noise got quieter. The path became clearer only after I started walking it.

That's when I realized I had to change the way I lived if I wanted to keep growing. I couldn't keep asking my mind for permission. My mind had proven it would always try to protect me by keeping me small.

So, I started practicing something simple. When I felt stuck, overwhelmed, or spiraling, I stopped thinking and started moving. I would set a timer for twenty minutes and just begin. No planning. No fixing. No perfecting. Just motion. Writing something messy. Making the call. Walking out the door. Saying yes before my fear could finish its sentence. And every time I did, something inside me loosened. It was like God met me halfway, but only once I took the first step. I started to see that movement itself was a form of trust. That maybe God wasn't asking me to be brave in my head, but faithful in my body.

When my thoughts began to spiral, I stopped sitting still trying to outthink them. I stood up. I walked. I stretched. I moved my body. I let motion interrupt the loop. And again and again, the same thing happened. My body calmed before my mind did. My breath slowed. The noise softened. Clarity came not through analysis, but through action.

I also had to learn to let things be imperfect on purpose. That one was hard. I had spent so much of my life believing that if I did something imperfectly, it would prove I wasn't enough. But I started practicing what I now think of as doing it dirty. Posting before it was polished. Speaking before I felt fully ready. Creating before I felt confident. It felt terrifying at first, like stepping out without armor. But every time I did it, the world didn't end. And neither did I.

Perfection had kept me frozen. Movement set me free.

Eventually, I made a rule for myself. If I had prayed about something for more than seven days, the next step was not more prayer. It was action. If God hadn't stopped me, redirected me, or closed the door, then the movement itself was the answer. I didn't need more signs. I needed to walk.

That was when I understood something I wish I had known earlier. Faith is not waiting until you feel ready. Faith is moving while you're still scared, trusting that God meets you in the motion.

I stopped asking, "What if I mess this up?" and started asking, "What if this is how I learn?" And slowly, quietly, without fireworks or certainty, my life began to shift. Not because I had it all figured out, but because I finally stopped standing still. I didn't need to know the whole path. I just needed to take the next step.

Journal Prompt: What action have I delayed out of fear of imperfection or failure? What "talent" have I buried instead of multiplying? What would it look like to move before I feel ready?

CHAPTER 9

YOU WERE NEVER MEANT TO CARRY IT ALONE

As I started applying more action with faith, my anxiety began to calm down temporarily as my life started to change right in front of my eyes. I was able to get a remote sales position, which meant I no longer had to stay tied to the same town filled with so much emotional weight and history. I could finally move. Explore. Breathe.

I backpacked through Peru and stood in awe at the ruins of Machu Picchu. I flew back to Portugal to see my close friend Andre and helped him with sales training again. And when my mom still held onto the hope that I might return to dental school, I shocked her by telling her I was buying a one-way ticket to Thailand. She completely lost it.

But I had fallen in love with faith paired with action. The more I moved, the more I trusted movement itself. The more I trusted it, the quieter my mind became at night. The noise softened. The spirals slowed. Motion gave me peace in a way that thinking never could.

From Thailand, I backpacked across Asia. Then I settled in Bali for four years. After that, I moved to Europe and bounced around for a while. I kept moving, almost as if motion itself was keeping me safe. I stayed in motion so my thoughts could not catch up to me. So the past could not catch me. So the fear could not sit down beside me.

But the devilish imp noticed.

He realized I wasn't listening to him anymore. I wasn't freezing or spiraling the way I used to. I wasn't obeying his fear scripts. And when he realized he was losing control, he adapted. He changed tactics. He waited for a moment when I was tired. When I was vulnerable. When I thought I had finally outrun him.

And when he came back, it hit harder than ever. So hard that it almost killed me.

You see, the funny thing about my personality is that it tends to be extreme. When I experience a certain level of pain in my life, I run hard in the opposite direction, convinced the answer must be there. And when living in that extreme works for a little while, like nonstop action mixed with blind faith and no thinking, I start to believe that this must be the cure for my anxiety and overthinking.

But the devilish imp is more cunning than that. It hides. It shape-shifts. It reaches into its bag of tricks and finds new ways to attack the mind. It waits patiently for a new opening.

In my case, my anxiety was deeply tied to money and relationships. My relationships suffered because of my lack of finances. So, in my mind, I created a simple equation. More money equals less anxiety. More money equals safety. More money equals peace.

I chased wealth, thinking it would save me. I thought money would protect me from pain. That if I just had enough, I would finally feel safe, respected, and free.

But what I slowly began to realize is that the devilish imp doesn't disappear just because your bank account grows. It simply changes costumes.

Between having no money and having an abundance of money, the devilish imp still has territory. It still finds ways in. It still whispers. It still feeds on fear.

I used to believe no money meant anxiety, and money meant peace. But if that were true, why did I watch people with more wealth than I could imagine still fall apart? Why did I see close friends and mentors, people who "had it all," still struggle so deeply that some of them tried to end their own lives?

I had a friend who recently tried to drown himself on purpose because his mind wouldn't stop racing. He couldn't quiet it. It all stemmed from a divorce. His wife had left him and taken the children because his chase for more and more wealth never stopped.

"Why?" I asked him. "Why did you try to end your life when you have so much?"

"Mike, you know that feeling you get when you don't have money?" he said. "That anxiety. That fear. That sense that you're not safe and you need more?"

"Yes," I responded.

"That feeling never leaves," he said. "It might go quiet for a few years. Maybe even a decade or two. But it always comes back. It never actually goes away."

I sat there in disbelief, slowly realizing just how cunning the devilish imp really is.

In my other book, *Longevity: The Chinese Secret to a Long and Happy Life*, I talk about a concept called the Dao. It's an ancient Chinese philosophy centered around balance. The harmony between opposites. The yin and the yang. The understanding that too much of anything, even something that seems good, eventually becomes destructive. Too much control. Too much ambition. Too much fear. Too much comfort. Too much striving. Too much of one thing is a bad thing.

For example, action plus faith is good. It saved me. But too much action and faith without stillness eventually leads to pride, and pride leads to envy, and envy leads to collapse. It can eventually lead to broken families. It can even lead to having kids who don't respect you because you were never *really* there. I have seen it over and over again. And I see it in myself whenever I start chasing wealth as the answer to the anxiety that lives inside me.

Oh, so maybe just being still is the answer, I thought.

Stillness is good. It brings reflection. Like the times my uncle told me that all he did was be still, and somehow everything worked itself out. Or the times when my body forced stillness onto me through sickness. GERD. Gastritis. An ulcer. Pneumonia. Or the time I was with someone I truly believed I would build a life with, only for her to spiral into a mental health crisis, in and out of psychosis, until circumstances and family differences ripped us apart.

In those moments, all I could do was be still. I couldn't fix it. I couldn't force it. I couldn't outwork it. And somehow, by doing nothing, things eventually got better.

However, I also learned that staying still for too long leads to passiveness. It leads to stagnation. It leads to fear pretending to be peace.

So, it's a dance. A constant movement between extremes. Between action and stillness. Between faith and rest. Between doing and surrendering. Back and forth. Over and over again. Bouncing back between the two as if you are balancing on one foot.

One thing I realized is that, in all of this movement, the devilish imp becomes clearer. I began to notice how it really takes control, how it manipulates, and how deeply it is connected to finances. I began to notice the pattern. The devilish imp evolves by approaching you from different angles, wearing different masks, often taking on the faces of the people you love and trust as you move between extremes.

That is what makes it so dangerous. The devilish imp doesn't always show up as something obviously evil. Sometimes it shows up wearing the face of someone you care about deeply. Someone whose voice you trust. Someone whose fears become your own.

Before my sales career ever took off, the devilish imp showed up wearing the faces of my mom and my dad. Their fears became my fears. Their anxieties became my anxieties. Their worries about money and stability soaked into me until they felt like my own thoughts. It felt like a generational curse. No matter how hard I tried, I couldn't escape it.

The devilish imp also shows up in relationships. Ones that may start healthy and full of promise. But when there is no clarity around values, no shared mission, no emotional boundaries, that relationship can turn toxic fast. It can slowly drain you without you realizing what is happening. Sometimes it comes in the form of a stranger who enters your life unexpectedly. You trust them. You open up. And then one day, you realize they were never safe people to confide in. You realize they are deeply narcissistic, and their only goal is control or validation at your expense.

The devilish imp has many disguises. It does not matter who you are, how old you are, how much money you make, or how little you have. If it cannot get to you through finances, it will try through relationships. If it cannot reach you through relationships, it will wait for you in the quiet hours of the night. It is patient. It adapts. It studies you.

The devilish imp constantly adapts.

So how do we ever fully break free from the devilish imp's grasp? How do we truly relieve our anxiety, stress, fear, and overthinking if this thing that lives in our mind is constantly on the attack? Of course, there is stillness. Of course, there is faith paired with action. But how do you know which one to use, and when? How do you know which mode is right for the moment you are in?

That's when it hit me. Why am I fighting this battle with the devilish imp alone?

I mean, I am not the only one feeling this pain. I am not the only one wrestling with these thoughts, these fears, this constant internal noise. There have to be others who feel this, too. I take a deep breath, and as I inhale, the truth lands in my chest.

I. Am. Not. Alone.

And yet, I had been living as if I was.

Why did I assume I had to fight this alone? Why did I believe that carrying this weight by myself was strength? That staying silent, holding it in, pushing forward without help was somehow noble?

That's when I realized something painful and freeing at the same time. Loneliness, isolation, keeping these thoughts trapped inside, refusing to speak them out loud, carrying the burden the devilish imp places on our shoulders in silence. That is not how we win. That is how we stay trapped.

That is how we keep running in circles. That is how the game never ends. This is how we constantly play the game of cat and mouse as we find ways to prevent the devilish imp from attacking our mind, as it adapts to whatever relief we find.

The secret that I found is being in a community where, whenever I am in a place of weakness, and the devilish imp seems to be winning, there is someone there. A brother. A sister. A close friend. A family member who understands the concepts of this book and understands the evil of the devilish imp. Someone who can call me out when I start spiraling.

It is accountability. It is a community. It is a village. It is what we lost in modern times as we became more individualistic, forgetting that societies only ever survived because of togetherness. Because of shared goals. Shared missions. Shared values.

My big problem was that I never defined what my mission or values were. Because of that, I kept finding myself in random friendships and relationships. I never realized that sometimes the devilish imp inside other people, whom they don't even know exists inside themselves, would awaken mine. Their unhealed wounds would feed my own. Their chaos would give my devilish imp more power.

The less aware the people around me were of their own devilish imps, the easier it was for me to forget that I had one, too. One is always waiting, always watching, ready to take control and push me into autopilot so it could steer my life toward suffering.

But when I surrounded myself with people who understood this inner battle, people who recognized the devilish imp and how it operates, something changed. When I was weak, they could see it before I could. They could call it out. They could shine a light on it when I forgot how. And in those moments, I would do the same for them when they were the ones slipping.

This is how it used to be. This is how humans survived. We stood together. We protected each other. We reminded one another who we were when we forgot.

But it's sad that we have forgotten just how powerful we are when we combine the same mission in life of togetherness, oneness, and being kind to one another while fending off the evils of the devilish imp's control and grasp.

As I sat with all of this, something slowly began to click inside me. I started to see that so much of my suffering was never about weakness. It was about isolation. I kept trying to carry things that were never meant to be carried alone. I kept trying to solve spiritual weight with mental effort. I kept believing that strength meant silence.

But it doesn't. I began to notice something strange. Every time I tried to carry everything by myself, the weight multiplied. But whenever I finally spoke it out loud to someone safe, something shifted. The fear didn't vanish, but it lost its grip. The anxiety didn't disappear, but it softened. It became manageable. Shareable.

That's when a verse I had heard before finally landed in my body, not just my mind.

"Carry each other's burdens, and in this way, you will fulfill the law of Christ." – Galatians 6:2.

I used to think that meant helping other people with their problems. Being strong for them. Being the one who could hold it together. I never realized it also meant letting others help carry mine.

Another verse started to make sense in a way it never had before. *"Two are better than one… If either of them falls, one can help the other up." – Ecclesiastes 4:9-10.*

I always thought that was about productivity or partnership. Like two people could get more done than one. But it's deeper than that. It's about survival. It's about the fact that when you fall inside your own mind, you cannot always get back up by yourself. Sometimes you need someone else to see you lying there and reach down before the darkness convinces you that staying down is easier.

And then there was this one. *"Confess your sins to one another and pray for one another so that you may be healed." – James 5:16.*

That one used to confuse me. Why would I tell someone else the things I'm ashamed of? Why would I expose the parts of me that already hurt? But I started to see it differently. Healing doesn't come from hiding the wound. It comes from letting light touch it. Silence keeps the infection alive. Exposure begins the healing.

Our culture teaches us to tough it out. To figure it out alone. To stay silent. To push through. To not need anyone. But that isolation isn't strength. It's a slow poison. A trap dressed up as independence.

I started to understand that God never designed us to carry everything alone. Not our fear. Not our shame. Not our doubts. Not our grief. Not our confusion. He built us for community. For brotherhood. For shared weight.

That realization hit me even deeper when I thought about the story of Moses. Moses was chosen. He was a leader. A prophet. A man who spoke directly with God. And yet, even he could not do it alone.

When the battle was raging, Moses stood on the hill with his arms raised. As long as his arms stayed up, his people were winning. But his arms grew tired. His strength failed him. And when his arms dropped, they began to lose.

So, what happened?

Two men stepped in. Aaron and Hur. They stood on either side of him and held his arms up. One on the left. One on the right. Not because Moses was weak, but because he was human. Victory didn't come from Moses trying harder. It came from shared strength. From shared burden. From shared faith.

That's when it finally clicked for me. I was never meant to hold my arms up alone. I was never meant to fight the devilish imp by myself. I was never meant to be my own savior, my own healer, my own anchor. I was meant to be part of something larger. A circle. A brotherhood. A sisterhood. A community that could see when my arms were shaking and step in before I collapsed. And that realization changed everything.

Modern Mindset vs. Biblical Wisdom

Modern Mindset	Biblical Wisdom
"Man up and deal with it."	"Carry each other's burdens." (Galatians 6:2)
"Don't show weakness."	"Confess your sins to one another." (James 5:16)
"You're alone in this."	"Where two or more gather in My name…" (Matthew 18:20)
"If you ask for help, you've failed."	"Even Moses needed help to lift his hands." (Exodus 17:12)
"Fix it yourself."	"Two are better than one." (Ecclesiastes 4:9)
"Isolation is strength."	"God sets the lonely in families." (Psalm 68:6)
"Figure it out on your own."	"Iron sharpens iron." (Proverbs 27:17)

I began to understand that if I wanted real freedom, I couldn't just rely on insight or willpower. I needed a structure that protected my heart when I was weak. I needed people who could see me clearly when I couldn't see myself at all. I needed habits that weren't about discipline for discipline's sake, but about staying connected to truth.

The first thing I learned was the power of brotherhood. Not surface-level friendships. Not people to grab drinks with or talk about work with. But men or women who actually loved God and were willing to tell me the truth, even when it made me uncomfortable. People who didn't flinch when I admitted fear or shame. People who didn't try to fix me right away, but sat with me long enough for the noise to settle. I realized how rare that kind of connection was, and how desperately I needed it. When I stopped trying to be impressive and started being honest, something softened inside me. I didn't feel so alone anymore.

Then I started practicing something that scared me at first. Vulnerability reps. Once a week, sometimes more, I would say out loud something I wanted to hide. A fear. A doubt. A temptation. A moment where I felt like I was slipping. Not to everyone. Just to someone safe. Someone grounded. Someone who could hold it without judging me or feeding it. I learned that shame thrives in silence, but it weakens when it's named. Each time I spoke it out loud, the grip loosened just a little more.

I also made a rule for myself that changed everything. I called it the "don't do it alone" rule. Any decision that touched my heart, my family, my future, or my faith could not be made in isolation. I had to run it by someone rooted in God. Not to ask for permission, but to gain perspective. To let someone else see my blind spots. I realized that most of my worst decisions were made in private, when I convinced myself I was being strong by carrying everything alone.

And then I committed to something simple but sacred. A check-in. A real one. Weekly or biweekly, depending on the season. A conversation where I didn't perform or pretend. Where I could say, "This is where I'm at. This is where I'm struggling. This is where I'm scared." And in return, I offered the same presence back. No fixing. No preaching. Just truth and care.

What surprised me most was how much lighter life became when I stopped trying to be self-sufficient. Strength stopped looking like control and started looking like connection. I wasn't weaker for needing others. I was finally human.

I began to see that God never intended for me to carry the weight of my life alone. He designed it so that healing would happen in the space between people. In shared silence. In honest words. In the courage to say, "I need help."

And slowly, as I practiced these habits, something shifted. The devilish imp still tried to whisper, but his voice wasn't as loud anymore. Because now, when he spoke, I wasn't listening alone. And that made all the difference.

Journal Prompt: What's one burden I've been carrying in silence? Financially, emotionally, spiritually? Why have I kept it hidden? What story do I believe about asking for help? Who is someone I trust that God may be calling me to open up to this week?

CHAPTER 10

THE MIND OF CHRIST

"I hate you, Mom." The sound of my own voice saying it felt like a punch to the chest. The words came out before I could stop them. Immediately, guilt and shame flooded my body. I didn't want to say it. I was afraid of saying it. I knew deep down I didn't mean it. But I let the words escape anyway as I slammed the pillow into the ground and cried, releasing all the pressure that had been sitting in my chest for so long.

After the screams left my body, sounding like the devilish imp was being exorcised from my soul, I lay there in a puddle of tears, wondering how I had ended up in this place.

I started thinking about where the anxiety first began to creep in. My partner and I had been having a lot of issues lately. At the beginning, everything felt healthy. There was respect. There was love. There were boundaries.

But as time went on and we grew closer, those boundaries slowly began to blur. And I noticed a familiar pattern emerging. The more time I spent with someone, the more I slipped into behaviors that felt normal to me. People-pleasing. Avoiding conflict. Not knowing how to say no. Offering my own suffering as proof of my love.

Every time I fell into that pattern, it allowed the other person's patterns to surface, too. And before I knew it, no matter how healthy or unhealthy their upbringing had been, every relationship began to follow the same script. It became toxic. Manipulative. Draining.

I didn't know how to express my needs or set boundaries, so I stayed. I stayed longer than I should have. I swallowed my discomfort. I said yes when I meant no. I smiled when I was breaking inside. And slowly, the anxiety began to build and build, until it lived in my chest permanently.

Without doubt, every single relationship would end up toxic and manipulative, with me not knowing how to express my needs or boundaries. I would remain in the relationship long enough for the anxiety to boil over in my mind, as the constant yeses and people-pleasing slowly destroyed all the respect I had for myself, both inside and out.

What usually triggers this pattern for me is money. Financial stress is almost always the doorway. There are certain things I can't say no to. Certain situations where, instead of choosing what is actually best for me, I people-please and bend so the other person can feel more comfortable. Over time, that builds resentment. It leaks out sideways. Passive aggression. Bitterness. Quiet anger directed at my partner, my friends, or whoever happens to be close enough to absorb it. Eventually, I fall into a victim mindset, telling myself that I am stuck, misunderstood, or taken advantage of.

I started to realize how deeply broken this pattern was, and I knew I had to get to the root of it. So, I spent money to attend an event in Bali that promised to help people "release" unresolved trauma. I didn't even fully know what that meant. I just knew I couldn't keep living the same way.

When I arrived, the event was held in a small boutique hotel overlooking the rice fields. The room was filled with people from all over the world, all wearing soft, loose white linen. They sat on plush, green, mosaic-like cushions spread across the floor. The air smelled like some kind of exotic incense, and the room felt unusually still. Quiet. Almost sacred.

I felt nervous. This was far outside my comfort zone. As I sat there, listening and observing, I started noticing the patterns in my own mind. The thoughts that kept surfacing. The same loops. The same fears. The same self-doubt. And I realized something uncomfortable. A lot of my identity, my anxiety, my fear, and my constant overthinking weren't actually mine to begin with.

They were inherited.

They came from my mom and my dad's nervous systems. From their fears. From their stress. From the way they saw the world. Their beliefs about money, love, success, sacrifice, and survival had quietly become mine. I had absorbed them before I even had the awareness to question them. Their self-talk became my self-talk. Their anxious worldview became the lens through which I saw life.

I began to understand that the devilish imp didn't just appear one day out of nowhere. Its power was built slowly, over time, through those inherited fears and thought patterns. It grew stronger every time I accepted those beliefs as truth without questioning them.

Many of my limiting beliefs, my fears, and my insecurities existed because that is secretly how my mom and dad felt about themselves.

And their self-talk and anxious worldview about money, love, success, and sacrifice became the foundation of my own nervous system. I absorbed it from the moment I was born, and it strengthened throughout my childhood. I never realized that this was where the devilish imp first gained its power, using those inherited thought patterns as fuel.

I knew this logically. But even knowing it, I found myself constantly falling back into the same patterns with money, relationships, my health, my people-pleasing, my lack of boundaries, and my fear of the future. All of it fed the same cycle. It only added more fuel to my anxious mind, sending it spiraling in every direction with no sense of control.

It was frustrating. I knew what my problem was. And yet I kept repeating it. I was addicted to my thoughts. Even though I could see them clearly, they still controlled me. That was the most terrifying part. And because of that, I decided to invest money into going to this event where I was supposed to learn how to "release" it all.

The way they described it made sense to me. Like a muscle that has been tight for so long that you forget what relaxed feels like. When someone finally massages it, it hurts at first. It's uncomfortable. But eventually, the tension releases, and your body remembers what ease feels like again. I realized my nervous system had never relaxed. Not once. Not since I was five years old.

So, there I was at the event. A woman with flowy blonde hair and a soft green sundress was leading the session. She had me sit in front of a pillow placed on the floor. Then she said something that made my chest tighten.

"Over the next thirty minutes, I want you to visualize your mom sitting on this pillow in front of you. She's not actually here. She's not even in the same country. But I want you to really see her as if she were right in front of you."

Then she continued.

"I also want you to visualize yourself as a five-year-old child. The child you were when you were hit by your dad. When you were told to be quiet. When you were told to be small. When you had to absorb the emotions of the room while your parents fought."

My throat tightened.

"Now," she said, "I want you to tell your mom everything you wish you could have told her when you were five. The things you never felt safe enough to say. The things you held inside because you thought your voice didn't matter. And I want you to say it while you hit the pillow in front of you."

I grimace. This feels weird. I really don't like sharing my emotions. And to say the things I secretly think, the things I have been ashamed to even admit to myself because I was afraid of hurting my mom, felt almost impossible.

But then I remembered my patterns. My anxious mind. The constant tension living in my chest. I didn't want to keep living like this. So I stayed open, and I tried. I hit the pillow softly, almost apologetically, like I was splashing water instead of striking something.

"Mom, I'm angry at you," I said quietly, my voice shaky and unsure.

Guilt wrapped around my throat like a hand trying to stop the words from coming out. Even though she wasn't in the room, the fear of hurting her felt unbearable.

"Hit the pillow and continue," the woman said.

"Mom, I'm angry that you control Dad."

I hit the pillow again, a little harder this time.

"More," the woman said.

"Mom, why are you so overbearing? Why are you so controlling? Why do you not give me space to breathe?"

I hit the pillow again, harder now. My body started to respond before my mind could stop it.

"More," she said again.

"Mom, why are you like this? I hate you. You're so controlling. You're so manipulative. You want to control my life. Why do you control Dad? Why are you so hard-headed? Why don't you care about your health? Do you want to die? Why are you throwing your health away? Can't you see that you're hurting me? Can't you see that you're hurting Dad? Can't you see that you're hurting yourself? Why do you do this? Why?"

The devilish imp was burning alive in my mind as I let everything spill out. Every word I had swallowed since I was five years old. Every thought I had buried because I was ashamed of it. Every feeling I told myself I wasn't allowed to have. I threw all of it onto that pillow.

And after a while, something strange happened. When you say a word over and over again, it starts to lose its power. When you express an emotion fully, without holding back, it starts to loosen its grip. The emotion of anger loses its charge.

After repeating my anger toward my mom for what felt like an eternity, I started to feel something strange. I began getting bored with the anger itself. The words lost their edge. I even tried swearing at her, cursing her, saying everything I could think of. But after a while, there was no more charge behind it. The anger stopped working. That's when the tears came. I realized that underneath the anger was sadness.

I hit the pillow softly.

"Mom, why do you do this?" I said quietly.

"Why are you like this? Why was it so painful?"

I cried for what felt like an eternity. I let out tears I had been holding in since I was five years old. I was a complete mess, but these weren't adult tears. These were the tears of a five-year-old boy who had to shove his feelings into strange corners of his soul just to survive. A little boy who learned early that expressing pain wasn't safe. I didn't realize then that when emotions aren't expressed, they don't disappear. They harden. They turn into scar tissue around the heart.

After I cried, something shifted. Underneath the sadness, I found understanding.

"Of course you're like this, Mom," I whispered. "How could you not be? Dad lost all his money and then married you. You had to raise my sister and me while he drank his depression away. You didn't feel safe. All you cared about was giving us a good life. You sacrificed your health, your relationship, your dreams, just so my sister and I could have a life you never had. You loved us so much that you sacrificed your own happiness and well-being for us."

And then, underneath that understanding, something else appeared.

Love.

Gratitude.

"I love you, Mom," I said softly. "I'm so grateful for you. I'm so blessed to have been born to such an amazing mother. I miss you. I'm sorry I was such a handful. I'm sorry I didn't listen. I'm sorry I caused you so much stress and heartache. I love you so much."

Pure love for my mom.

The love and gratitude were always there. They had just been buried beneath layers of anger and sadness that were never expressed. It was just suffocated by the levels of anger and sadness unexpressed that never let the love and gratitude have their time and place in the day.

I did the same thing with my dad. I visualized him sitting there in front of me. I tried to see if there was any anger there. Even when nothing came up at first, I kept going. I let my mouth start talking, letting words come out just to get the process moving.

"Dad, why don't you know how to set boundaries?" I said, snot still running down my nose, not fully recovered from the conversation with my mom.

"Dad, why do you constantly drink? Dad, why did you hit me when I was younger? Why did you lock me in rooms? Why did you hit me with a belt? Why did you throw trash on my bed to wake me up?"

The momentum started to build.

"Dad, why did you give up on your dreams? Why weren't you better at saving money? Why are you so bad with finances? Dad, why didn't you divorce Mom? Why did you stay? Because of you, I people please now. I stay in relationships that are toxic and manipulative because you didn't have the strength to say no."

I let it all out. The same process again. Anger unleashed, pouring out all the vengeance that had been trapped inside me since I was five years old.

Then came the sadness.

"Dad, I feel so sad. You sacrificed your dreams of entrepreneurship because you had me. You gave up your goals just to raise a son and a daughter. You gave up all your friends and moved to a new country just to suffer so that I could have a better life."

I cry, realizing just how much pain my dad was in.

"Of course you drank. I mean, how could you not? With a wife who was overbearing and controlling like Mom, what else were you supposed to do? Of course, you escaped. Why would you want to spend time in a house filled with yelling, fighting, and crying children?"

I cry even more as I realize just how much hardship my dad went through.

"Of course, you play it safe now. You lost so much money when you were younger that the trauma nearly destroyed you. You almost didn't want to live. And then you had children. Of course, you didn't want to make that same mistake again."

Understanding turns into love. Love turns into gratitude.

"Dad, I love you. All I want is for you to live a long life without stress. You deserve peace. You deserve happiness. I love you so much for taking the time to teach me things. For bringing me along when you went door to door doing sales. You taught me so many things that shaped the man I am today, and I wouldn't change a single thing about you or the childhood you gave me. I am blessed to have you as my father. I love you."

"I'm sorry for being such a difficult son. I'm sorry I didn't tell you I loved you more often. Dad, I want a new relationship with you and Mom. I want us to be a happy family. Dad, I want to take away all your financial burdens so that you and Mom can focus on loving each other as you did in those wedding videos I saw from before I was born."

"Dad, you can finally relax now. It's my turn to take the mantle."

I hug my knees into my chest, visualizing my mom and dad in front of me, and the five-year-old boy who never had a voice, now finally strong enough to understand just how much pain his mom and dad were in. It was in that moment that the identity given to me by my parents, the one that had been absorbed and twisted by the devilish imp, was finally released.

I could feel it leaving my body. The hurt, anxious mind of that five-year-old child, carrying unprocessed trauma that turned into years of stress, fear, and overthinking, began to soften. And in its place, something new arrived. Love. Gratitude.

Love and gratitude for my family. Love and gratitude for the people who stayed. Love and gratitude for the people who showed me kindness. Love and gratitude even for the people who hurt me. Love and gratitude toward God. Love and gratitude for the life I've been given.

And in that moment, I realized that even in the most painful and traumatic experiences, I no longer had to harden my heart the way I always had before. Instead of bracing, I could soften. Instead of armouring myself, I could open. No matter what challenges came my way, I could meet them with love rather than fear.

That love and gratitude became an antidote. Something that washed through the anxiety when it tried to return. Something that soothed the parts of me that once believed survival meant staying tense and guarded.

When all that guilt, shame, fear, anger, and pain finally loosened their grip, space opened inside of me. Space for something new. Space for peace. Space for truth. And in that space, a new identity began to form. An identity that was given to us by God when we have a calm mind.

And that's when something inside me finally clicked. I began to realize that God wasn't just trying to calm my mind. He was trying to replace it. I had spent so much of my life trying to manage my thoughts, regulate my anxiety, quiet the noise, and negotiate with fear. I thought healing meant learning how to cope better. How to tolerate the chaos without falling apart. But what I was starting to see was that God was offering something much deeper than coping.

"Let this mind be in you which was also in Christ Jesus." – Philippians 2:5. I had heard that verse before, but it never landed until now. I always assumed it meant "try to think like Jesus," as if it were some moral upgrade or mindset hack. But sitting there, after everything I had just

released, I realized something different. God wasn't asking me to improve my thinking. He was offering to replace the system entirely.

My mind had been running on an operating system built from fear, survival, performance, and shame. It made sense why it kept breaking down. It was designed in trauma. It learned safety through control. It learned love through approval. It learned worth through usefulness.

And God wasn't interested in tweaking that system. He wanted to give me a new one. That's when I realized that the mind of Christ isn't reactive. It doesn't scramble for control. It doesn't panic when things feel uncertain. It doesn't need to perform to feel worthy.

It rests. It trusts. It listens. And that terrified me at first, because I realized how much of my identity was built on tension. On striving. On proving. On staying ahead of pain. Who would I be without all that noise?

That's when the story of Saul came to mind. Before he became Paul, Saul was driven by fear disguised as righteousness. He needed control. He needed certainty. He needed to be right. He believed he was serving God, but he was really serving his own need to feel safe and significant. And then everything stopped. *"Immediately, something like scales fell from Saul's eyes." – Acts 9:18.*

It wasn't just his sight that changed. His entire inner world was rebuilt. The same man, but with a completely different operating system. The one who once hunted now healed. The one who once destroyed now carried love. God didn't just redirect him. He redefined him. That's when it hit me. I wasn't broken. I was just running an old system. A system built by fear, survival, and inherited trauma. By voices that were never mine to begin with. And God wasn't asking me to fix it. He was asking me to lay it down. To stop trying to outthink my fear and instead let Him think through me. To stop trying to manage life and start trusting the One who already holds it.

"You have the mind of Christ." – 1 Corinthians 2:16. Not someday. Not when you're healed enough. Not when you finally get it together. Now.

That realization didn't come with fireworks. It came with a quiet sense of relief. Like setting down a weight I didn't realize I had been carrying my whole life. I didn't need to know everything anymore. I didn't need to predict every outcome. I didn't need to protect myself from every possible pain. I just needed to stay connected. To let my thoughts be filtered through truth instead of fear. To let love interrupt my reflexes. To let grace rewrite my reactions. That was the beginning of real freedom. Not control. Not certainty. Not perfection. But trust. And for the first time, I understood that the mind of Christ isn't something you achieve. It's something you receive.

Modern Mindset vs. Biblical Wisdom

Modern Mindset	Biblical Wisdom
"Improve your mindset."	"Let this mind be in you which was in Christ." (Philippians 2:5)
"Think positive."	"Be transformed by the renewing of your mind." (Romans 12:2)
"Shift your thoughts."	"You have the mind of Christ." (1 Corinthians 2:16)
"Calm your anxiety."	"Perfect love casts out fear." (1 John 4:18)
"You're in control."	"Trust in the Lord with all your heart..." (Proverbs 3:5)
"Train your mindset like a muscle."	"Unless a man is born again..." (John 3:3)
"Manage your mind."	"Receive the mind of Christ."

That realization changed how I began to live day to day. I stopped trying to "fix" myself through force and started learning how to *receive* a different way of being. Not through striving. Not through discipline alone. But through surrender practiced daily, gently, and intentionally.

I started with silence. Not the kind where you're waiting for noise to stop, but the kind where you actually sit with yourself long enough to notice what's moving underneath. In those moments, I would imagine Christ sitting with me, not above me, not disappointed, not correcting me. Just present. Calm. Steady. I would picture Him offering me His mind the way someone offers a hand. His peace. His clarity. His compassion. His quiet authority. And I would let myself receive it, even if only for a few seconds at first. I wasn't trying to become someone else. I was learning to rest inside something truer.

Then I began to notice how loud my inner voice still was throughout the day. The fear. The self-doubt. The old reflex to brace for impact. So, I started meeting those thoughts with new words. Not affirmations meant to hype me up, but truths meant to ground me. When fear rose, I'd say quietly, "I am not afraid." When shame crept in, "I am not condemned." When my mind spiraled, "I am not alone." When I felt small, "I am chosen." When I felt broken, "I am a new creation." I didn't say them to convince myself. I said them to remember who I already was.

And slowly, something shifted.

Whenever a fear-based thought tried to take over, I stopped wrestling with it. I didn't argue with it or analyze it. I simply named it for what it was and replaced it. I would tell myself, "That's not who I am anymore. I have the mind of Christ." Not as a denial of pain, but as a declaration of identity. The thought didn't disappear instantly, but it lost its authority. It no longer got to decide what was true.

There were moments when the old patterns flared up hard. When anxiety surged through my body before I could catch it. In those moments, I learned a simple exchange. I would pause and say, "Jesus, I lay this thought down. I don't want to carry it anymore. Give me Yours instead." Sometimes, that meant peace. Sometimes, clarity. Sometimes, just enough stillness to breathe again. But every time, something softened.

What I began to understand was this: healing wasn't about silencing my mind. It was about choosing which voice I trusted. My old mind spoke in urgency, fear, and self-protection. The mind of Christ spoke in patience, truth, and safety.

And over time, something beautiful happened. My default response began to change. I didn't spiral as quickly. I didn't brace for impact as often. I didn't need to control every outcome to feel okay. I started living from a place of being held instead of holding everything together myself.

That's when I realized these weren't just habits. They were acts of surrender. Daily invitations to let God think through me instead of me trying to survive on my own understanding. And little by little, the old noise lost its grip. The fear loosened. The urgency softened. Not because life became easier, but because I was no longer facing it alone. I wasn't just managing my mind anymore. I was learning to live from a new one.

Journal Prompt: What fear-based thoughts still control how I see myself, others, or the future? Where did those thoughts begin? In childhood, through rejection, through trauma?

CHAPTER 11

WHEN THE MIND FINALLY LEARNS TO REST

If you made it here, you didn't just read a book. You walked through your own mind. You traced the loops, the spirals, the questions that never seemed to land anywhere. You followed the thoughts that kept you up at night, the ones that replayed conversations, mistakes, futures that hadn't happened yet. You sat with the part of you that never stops thinking, planning, bracing, preparing. And somewhere along the way, something shifted.

You began to see that the problem was never that you think too much. It's that you were trying to think your way into safety.

Most of your life, your mind learned that overthinking was protection. If you stayed alert, you wouldn't get hurt. If you analyzed every angle, you wouldn't be blindsided. If you replayed every conversation, maybe you could finally get it right next time. Overthinking became your armor. Your early warning system. Your attempt at control. But armor gets heavy when you never take it off. What you're learning now is that peace doesn't come from better thinking. It comes from a different *source* of thinking altogether.

The mind of Christ doesn't spiral. It doesn't catastrophize. It doesn't rehearse shame. It rests in truth. And that's why this journey was never about fixing your overthinking. It was about outgrowing the identity that needed overthinking to feel safe.

You're starting to notice it now. The thoughts still come, but they don't hook you the same way. The fear still whispers, but it doesn't own you. The mind still speaks, but it no longer gets the final word. And the moment you start to let go of control, you realize that overthinking loses its power the moment you stop believing it's you.

You are not your thoughts. You are the one noticing them. And that awareness changes everything.

You will still have days when your mind races. You will still wake up some mornings with tension in your chest or questions you can't answer yet. That doesn't mean you're failing. It means you're human. But now you know what to do when it happens. You pause. You soften. You return. You remember that peace isn't something you chase. It's something you allow. You remember that clarity comes not from force, but from stillness. You remember that God is not asking you to figure everything out. He is inviting you to rest in Him while He does the shaping.

"He who began a good work in you will carry it on to completion." – Philippians 1:6. You don't have to finish this journey today. You don't have to solve your whole life. You just have to stay open.

The overthinking mind learns to quiet not by being silenced, but by being understood. And in that understanding, something sacred happens. The noise fades. The grip loosens. The heart softens. And in the stillness, you realize you were never broken. You were becoming. This isn't the end. It's the beginning of a mind that finally knows how to rest.

BEFORE YOU GO… A SMALL GIFT

Thank you for walking with me through these pages. This book was never meant to be a one-time read. It's meant to be practiced slowly, quietly, and daily, until peace becomes your default posture instead of panic. But I also know the journey doesn't end here.

So, I created something to support you beyond the book: a collection of simple, printable tools to help keep your mind anchored when the spiral tries to return.

These are **completely free**, created just for readers like you:

What's Inside Your Free Toolkit:

1. **The Morning Stillness Reset:** A 5–10-minute daily ritual to quiet mental noise before it takes over. Includes breath guidance, Scripture, and grounding reflection to help you begin the day in peace instead of pressure.
2. **The Nighttime Release Ritual:** A calming, step-by-step evening practice to unload stress, release mental loops, and signal safety to your nervous system so you can rest deeply.
3. **The Overthinking Interruption Guide:** Short, practical prompts to use in the moment when your thoughts start spiraling. Designed to help you recognize fear-based thinking and gently replace it with truth.
4. **Fear-to-Faith Reflection Journal:** Ten guided journal prompts rooted in Scripture to help you uncover the fears

driving your overthinking and reframe them through faith, compassion, and clarity.

5. **Relationship & Boundary Clarity Pages:** Gentle, honest questions to help you identify people-pleasing patterns, emotional overextension, and the moments you abandon yourself to keep the peace.
6. **Weekly Peace Check-In:** A simple one-page weekly reflection to track emotional patterns, notice growth, and reconnect with the calm you are learning to live from.

You can download everything here
mikevestil.com/overthinking-gift
(or scan the QR code below)

These are yours. Use them. Carry them. Print and share them with someone you love.

They're not a replacement for Scripture; they're a companion. They're tools to help you do what this book invited you into: **one breath, one prayer, one peaceful thought at a time.**

You're not alone in this. And you don't have to be perfect to walk in peace. You just have to practice.

CAN I ASK YOU SOMETHING SMALL?

If this book met you in a moment when your mind was loud, your chest was tight, or your thoughts were spiraling at 3 a.m., and if even one page helped you feel still again, even for a breath... Would you take 60 seconds to share that?

Reviews aren't just stars on Amazon. They're **small lanterns** for the next person scrolling in the dark, exhausted, and looking for peace. Your words might be the very thing that helps someone else feel seen.

You don't need to write much. A sentence or two about what connected with you is more than enough.

You can simply scan the QR code below or go to this link:
mikevestil.com/overthinking-review
(or scan the QR code below)

I read every single one. And I carry your words with me, just like I hope you'll carry some of these pages with you. Thank you for walking this road with me. You matter more than you know.

AFTERWORD: THE JOURNEY CONTINUES

If you've made it to the final page, you didn't just finish a book; you made a quiet, courageous choice to face what's been chasing you. To stop running from the noise. To walk through the spiral… and not let it own you anymore.

And maybe, for the first time in a long time, you let yourself breathe. This wasn't meant to be another self-help manual. It was meant to feel like a hand on your shoulder at 3 a.m. A rhythm. A companion. A quiet space to come home to yourself and to God.

Because I know what it's like to lie in the dark with a loud mind. To feel the ache of pretending everything's fine while you're unraveling inside. To live in your head, rewriting the past, fearing the future, and wondering…

"Is peace even possible for someone like me?"

Let me say this clearly: Yes. It is.

You don't have to fix everything to be worthy of rest. You don't have to figure it all out to be loved. You don't have to carry it all to be strong. Sometimes the holiest thing you can do… is stop trying to be God. And let yourself be held by Him instead.

If there's anything I pray you carry from these pages, it's this:

- You don't have to earn peace by perfecting yourself.
- You don't have to prove your worth through endless performance.

- You don't have to think your way into healing.
- You are allowed to rest.
- You are allowed to ask for help.
- You are allowed to live lightly.

This journey isn't over. It never really is. But now, you have tools. Now, you know where to return when the spiral starts again. Now, you know whose mind you carry, not your old one, but the **mind of Christ**. So come back to these truths when the noise returns. You are not the sum of your anxious thoughts. You are not what fear says about you.

You are who God calls you: *Beloved. Renewed. Safe. Not alone.*

If this book helped you in any way, please consider sharing it. Because somewhere right now, someone is scrolling in silence, searching for something that feels like hope. Your simple act of passing this along may be the lifeline they've been praying for.

With all my hope and peace for you,

Mike Vestil

P.S. I'd love to hear from you. If you have thoughts, questions, or just want to say thank you, email me anytime: hello@mikevestil.com. I read every message.

ABOUT THE AUTHOR

MIKE VESTIL

I'm not a therapist, pastor, or mental health expert. I'm the son of immigrants, a former perfectionist, and a recovering overthinker. And for a long time, I believed peace was something you had to *earn*. I thought if I planned enough, succeeded enough, and kept everyone happy enough, maybe the spirals would stop. Maybe I'd finally sleep through the night. But the truth was: the more I tried to control everything, the more I lost myself.

The turning point wasn't loud. It was quiet. A season of exhaustion. A collapsed body. An anxious mind. A soul I had neglected for too long. That's when God met me, not with lightning, but with stillness. Not with answers, but with **presence**.

I began learning that peace doesn't come from figuring everything out. It comes from **surrender**. From trusting the One who holds what I can't.

This book wasn't written from a mountaintop; it was written from the valley. From late nights, hard prayers, and slowly learning that *overthinking is not the voice of wisdom, it's the voice of fear pretending to be in control.*

Today, I live a slower life across the world in Asia, rooted in faith, family, and a rhythm of peace that no longer depends on productivity or performance. I've traded my frantic "figure it out" energy for daily trust. Not perfectly. But faithfully.

This book is for those whose minds run faster than their faith. For those tired of trying to think their way into peace. For those who lie awake wondering if they're the only ones.

You're not alone. You're not broken. And you don't have to carry it all anymore.

I don't write this as a guru. I write this as a brother who's still learning to be still.

Stay connected:

mikevestil.com: writings, reflections, and occasional updates Instagram: @mikevestil

www.ingramcontent.com/pod-product-compliance
Lightning Source LLC
LaVergne TN
LVHW051005080826
845145LV00009B/2470

* 9 7 8 1 9 6 9 6 7 5 0 8 9 *